Single Rising From Ashes

Starting Over in the Singles Dating World

Lynn Lasso

Single Rising From Ashes!

Print ISBN: 979-8-9923951-0-5

Thank You!

Thank you to the Lord who reached out to me when I was broken and wanted to give up, He empowered me to take my first step, leading me down this book's path.

Jim & Darlene Fuqua
Shug & Mom.
My extreme gratitude for your support and for preparing me for this journey,
including charm school!
And the great family life that you have provided.

Heather & Jace Dockery
The best daughter and Grandson.
Constantly mindful of my time and encouraging me to write.

Madeline Wise
My friend who always believed in me and placed the "write cup" on my desk.

Contents

"Be the Prize"

"I can do all things through Christ who strengthens me" (Phil 4:13)

Chapter 1

My Story

I HAVE WALKED a similar journey to yours and want to share my comeback to help you see your possibilities and encourage you to care for yourself while building a better life. Don't leave yourself at the end of the line. You are valuable and worthy!

Seven years ago, an ambulance took me to the hospital the morning after I'd fallen and broken a glass tabletop. I lay unconscious on the floor of glass until Thursday morning when my sister called and awakened me.

The emergency room nurse described the medical tests needed for my diagnosis and treatment while inquiring about how I came to be in this condition. On the previous Monday, I had a minor infection treated with antibiotics. By late Wednesday, the infection appeared drug-resistant, and another antibiotic was prescribed. Because of the late hour, I waited until Thursday morning to pick up the antibiotic. Thursday was too late!

I told her, "My life is crap. I feel like crap." I declined the tests as I had reached the point when I didn't want to hurt mentally or physically anymore. She brought my daughter, a nurse, from the waiting room. My daughter leaned over me, forcing me to listen, and said, "Mom, you are dying at this minute. Your blood pressure is 42 over 38. You need to figure out if you want to live or die. Your grandson and I need you."

I saw visions of my daughter and grandson living without me because I was too beat up to fight my way back. She then turned to the nurse and said, "Give Mom the tests as recommended and ignore her complaints."

I nodded in agreement with the treatment plan. My beautiful daughter stood in the gap between life and death, encouraging me to rebuild my life. That day, I embraced my healing.

Through my divorce, I lost myself and forgot how to smile, which was my most used expression. I gained weight and lost my feelings of self-worth in the days leading up to the hospital awakening. I could no longer remember what I liked, where to go, or the music I enjoyed listening to. Even though my family and friends surrounded me, I was lonely.

If I were to live, I needed to create a plan to restore my health. My wounds were in *my mind, body, and soul,* requiring an all-inclusive strategy. My mind was foggy, and I could not think or access skills gleaned from a lifetime of work experience or grand education. The retention of even two letters of my computer password was gone. The most minor decisions were tough.

My lack of sleep was caused by the trauma of divorce, the stress of the business transition, and my inability to shut down my negative thoughts. I began productive sleep around ten p.m. with the help of a giant margarita. The alcohol helped me with the sleep problem until it burned off near midnight. Then, I watched television until I fell asleep again between three and five in the morning. To make matters worse, I lost my sense of day/night rhythm. For these reasons, including depression, I could not dream, even though I needed strength for a better life.

When I met with my therapist, my first words to her were, "I'm crazy." She disagreed and helped me analyze where I was in my life and to understand my state of mind. She asked many questions but did not tell me how to feel or to change my attitude. Her questions helped me clarify my thoughts about my present, my past, and my future.

She gave me insights into seeing my past life differently, being more positive about my present, and working toward a better future. Finding help was like finding a compass pointing north where I could determine my future direction.

My mind was still not free of the torments of the negative record playing. Negative thoughts and second-guessing myself had become the norm, and fresh thoughts and activities needed to replace the negative ones.

At that point, I began eliminating everything harmful from my life. I turned off the news and avoided negative relationships and conversations. I purposely listened to upbeat music and played it constantly, almost like a chant. I played songs for the healing words and calming melodies.

The lyrics comforted me. Some tunes were new, and some were old, but positivity was the common thread. As I listen to the old song "What a Wonderful World" by the late, great singer Louie Armstrong, I see visions of green trees, blue skies, rainbows, and babies crying. I listen to the song repeatedly and envision happiness. Flooding my mind with positive, wholesome thoughts drowned out the struggles and past failures.

Another of my favorite songs was "The Greatest Love of All" by Whitney Houston. The lyrics contained meaningful words like fulfillment, acknowledging failure, and encouragement to create our path. As the words build, I was reminded of the greatest love that lives within us. It enabled me to find the strength to resist negative thoughts and activities. This was the beginning of my plan for finding control and peace in my mind. My faith gave me the strength and power to move ahead.

Walking two to four miles daily to the sounds and words of these songs was freeing and peaceful. Internalizing and visualizing every word left no space for negativity to creep in. I also worked out three days a week. Building strength and stamina allowed me to resume playing golf, pickleball, and more.

I reinvented myself and my attitude, changing how my body looked and felt while recapturing my health. The new body needed a new look: wardrobe, hair, and makeup.

Those changes helped me reestablish myself, gain new confidence, and add a boost my step.

My smile is back, and so is my fun-loving demeanor. I am proof that others have gone through hell and have found a life worth living.

THE FOLLOWING IS a client sharing her return from a terrible life experience.

To Escape the Smoke, I Jumped into a Narcissist's Flame

"Lynn found me living through a horrible situation. A narcissist had destroyed my self-esteem, work, and confidence. I had been both financially and emotionally manipulated and depleted. I desperately needed the beacon of hope Lynn selflessly gave to me. As if an angel, Lynn took me under her wing.

After three years of coaching and friendship, I am a very confident woman thanks to Lynn's empathy, compassion, and knowledge of relationships. Now, I can take on what life hands me, good or bad. Everyone needs a positive cheerleader in their life.

Lynn has a gift that very few people have. In her exciting

new book, she explains how to recognize and solve very personal conflicts."

J.J. Fresno, CA.

The new life you create will be faithful to you.
Deliberate, focused, and through mature eyes.

Seek peace in every area of your life,
nurture positive relationships,
create good boundaries and find your joy!

Chapter 2

Grief & Mourning

BECOMING SINGLE, by death or divorce, causes us to grieve. The grieving process takes as long as it takes. For some people, grief lasts a few months and for others much longer. Grief is the emotional response to the loss of a loved one.

Many people begin the grieving process even before a death due to the anticipation of an upcoming loss. An example is when we grieve for the loss of health. For instance, your mate had a heart attack that caused lifestyle limitations. Once an avid hunter, now he or she is limited to checkers in a rehabilitation home.

Early on, we may deny the loss ever happened, as we pretend or think, "When I wake up in the morning, this will just be a bad dream."

You may become angry with yourself, others, and even the victim, saying, "If only I hadn't made him go to the store, he would still be here." Or, "If I'd made her go to the doctor earlier, she could have been saved." You might even bargain everything you own to have your loved one's health restored.

My dad had a brain tumor, and when the life-altering prognosis was discovered, my grandfather sought to bargain his life for my dad's. Grandfather stated that he had a long enough life and suffered from poor health caused by diabetes and felt his life was hopeless. He questioned the Lord, "Why couldn't the Lord take him and leave my dad?" Other negotiations might be begging God by saying, "Take me, the kids need their mom." But that is not the way life works.

Depression is real and symptoms may include not wanting to eat or get dressed. Therefore, not allowing others to visit you or you visiting others. You might begin to withdraw or isolate yourself from everything you love to do.

You or a loved one may feel emotionally numb and cannot conceive the loss could occur. You are anxious as if you need to do something but don't know how to start. "I'll do it tomorrow." Yet, that day never comes, and you still mourn.

Most mental health writings say not to make any drastic decisions until after the one-year anniversary following a loss, death, or divorce. The first year following loss is an emotional time. Decisions made during this time are often based on feelings instead of sound reasons. You need time for personal healing but everyone heals in their own way. A man proposed to me two months after he lost his wife.

Consider grief groups who hike, take trips together, and offer support when others cannot. Many churches have grief groups and singles classes providing camaraderie to people in similar situations.

"By 25 months after the spouse's death, 61% of men and 19% of the women were either remarried or involved in a new romance." (Schneider, et al.)

You may be asking, "What does the death and grieving process have to do with a book about being single and your single life?" As it turns out, your grief stage has a lot to do with your ability to move forward and reestablish a new life.

After trying to live in a quiet house and feeling restless, you recognize the need to move your life forward but have no idea how. Eating and waking up alone with no one to talk with leaves you feeling empty. The need to be held seems greater than ever before. We want someone to fix our lives, but there is nobody there. Maybe you are not necessarily seeking sex but the comfort of being held.

Men have an especially high rate of remarriage or getting into long-term relationships within the first year. In fact, I had three men ask me to marry on the first date. Why? I'm not special, these men were trying to replace their loved one. I have talked with many widowers, good men, and my usual answer when asked about marriage is, "Let's talk about that next year."

Combine the drive that overcomes you due to the loneliness, the need to be held, and the want of a physical release. These traits tend to motivate us to date again. When you were young, bars and churches were traditional places to meet prospective mates, but the bar culture has changed. A great choice for finding a new mate is through family or friends.

Online dating has also become a popular way of meeting people and as a means to find potential mates. Online dating is seldom as simple as registering your profile on Monday and meeting Mr. or Ms. Wonderful on Saturday night. Finding a prospect who has similar interests is like finding a needle in a haystack. Look at other places as well, like hobbies and interests where you can meet like-minded people with a similar physical ability to congregate.

Wineries have become increasingly popular places to meet people, as they are attracting Las Vegas-quality acts locally. Pickleball is an upcoming sport for all ages. It's like tennis but less running. Go ride a horse. Go hiking! Try something, even if you fail.

Think about donating your time to a cause that you believe in. Cut the neighbors' grass, fix a fence, visit rest homes, and join community groups, as doing for others gives fulfillment. To move forward in our lives and seek optimism, we need to control our busy minds by filling them with positive experiences. Helping others makes the misery of finding a new life a little easier.

Get out of the house and get a life!
When you get involved, you build and move
toward accepting your new life.

Chapter 3

Loneliness

ADULTS AND CHILDREN EXPERIENCE LONELINESS. The feelings of aloneness make us feel empty, detached, and unwanted. I felt lonely in a crowd of 1,000 people, with friends, and alone at home.

Loneliness is not just about being alone; it is about feeling lonely. Some of our behaviors, like hiding away in our homes, add to our lonely feelings. The lack of a social connection makes us feel like a ship at sea without an anchor or direction. Our daily routine has been interrupted. Our lives have a void; we seek something to fill that space. What do we do with all this time on our hands?

Often, people fill the time trying to drown out the loneliness with alcohol and the bar scene. For those who never indulged in alcohol, severe increases in alcohol consumption are common. Prolonged loneliness can be detrimental to one's health.

I was a textbook case of loneliness and depression. During that time, I made some terrible decisions and learned to live with them. I had even lost my smile, which was my regular expression.

I sought the source of my depression to overcome the extreme pain and stopped the bedtime margaritas. Instead, I began a daily regimen including a two-mile walk, crunches, leg lifts both at home and the gym. Exercise made me tired and I slept better. The exercise occupied my mind and body, even if it was just for a few minutes. And for my soul, I prayed not just for a new life, but for a new way to live life.

I got involved with some charities, including a local hospital. I prayed and removed everything negative from my life. I had already tried every way I dreamed of to make myself happy but found no happiness.

However, I found contentment and hugs from the families of the critically ill in the hospital/family housing. My need to be held was satisfied through volunteering. This was a more satisfying outlet than bars. I can only imagine where I would be now if I had taken another path.

When we go through the loss process we don't know where to go or what to do with ourselves. We often hang out with our parents or kids, day after day, month after month. This is good for a season but at some point, we need to learn to create our own lives. While we spend time with the kids, we avoid facing our lives and problems. Family and friends have lives, and our constant presence interrupts their daily routine.

We've all heard the old saying, "Garbage-in, Garbage-out." So, be careful of what we think and internalize. Garbage-in: negative thoughts and failures used to beat us up rather than build ourselves up by celebrating small and large victories. I decided not to let negativity in my life and started walking with positive music. Learn to be your best friend!

Don't suffer in silence. Reach out!!!

Tell someone that you are having a hard time coping. If you are having thoughts of ending your life or hurting yourself Call 988

The National Suicide Prevention Lifeline, Substance abuse and mental Health Line by Texting "HOME" to 741741 (Downloaded 10/23/2023)

The lack of treatment also causes death!

Think about this and the pain it will cause those who love you!

*I have traveled along that path;
I know where you are!*

*Try life one more time for me!
Love you, Lynn*

Chapter 4

Living in the Void

THE VOID IS DESCRIBED as an empty space with no value, lacking and abandoned. When we cannot bare to spend another moment alone our thoughts may spiral. Coming to grips with the void in your life can look like this.

My dad died before Thanksgiving 1990, and the Thanksgiving holiday dinner had a terrible absence. By Christmas, I was sure I could not face Christmas dinner in our traditional way, and family time had to be something more.

My sister, daughter, and I, visited convalescent homes on Christmas morning before dinner festivities. My sister served cookies to residents who were very ill, immobile, and without visitors.

The Void From Another's Point of View

KH (Central Valley, CA)

"I was in my mid-50s, blessed with wonderful friends, a loving family, three amazing granddaughters, and a successful career. Even with all this, I felt myself spiraling downward. I could no longer find fun in life or appreciate what I had accomplished. I was not in a good place emotionally, physically, or spiritually. Every day there was a grind.

I felt stuck and aimless and had no clue how to find the next steps to gain clarity and get unstuck. I was throwing myself into my work, becoming a workaholic. I found myself using alcohol as a crutch to numb the pain of what I felt had become a meaningless existence. My health was becoming seriously at risk. I felt invisible when it came to the opposite sex, feeling hopeless that the chance for love may have escaped the second half of my life. Feelings of unattractiveness and unworthiness weighed heavily on me.

Then I found Lynn. It's a funny story, really. My adult children were at a festival and saw her booth. They thought "Geez, this is what Mom needs!" and signed me up. I had no clue who she was when she called and was baffled by how she knew so much about me. It took me a minute to figure out that my kids were at the bottom of this intervention.

After working with Lynn, her calming presence helped me to get my life back on track. She encouraged me to get back up and keep trying. She inspired me to identify my priorities, redefine my goals, and set healthy boundaries. Her guidance allowed me to gain clarity and again discover the potential I had inside of me.

I've reconnected with my Faith and with myself regaining my enthusiasm for life. I now find moments of fun and joy in the everyday moments of my life. My mindset has changed to one of gratitude and positivity. My life has transitioned to one of gladness and satisfaction.

Today my life feels meaningful once again and is full and wonderful. I have dropped pounds, found activities I love, and am well on my way to a healthier me. The most beautiful change is because of the head-start Lynn gave me, I was ready for and have found love again. Thank you!"

As long as you have breath and are free from bed, you can change your life!

May your Christmas dinner have a new meaning, as mine did the year after the hollow Thanksgiving.

Chapter 5

Single, Now What?

Like the Marine Corps, we only need a few good men and women!

BUILDING a new community of friends and potential partners requires a positive attitude. Embracing a new mindset opens doors to healthy change. When I smile, it seems everyone smiles back at me, thus demonstrating a smile is contagious. We create an impact on others as we greet them by either attracting or detracting. A new attitude will heavily contribute to your success. To gain a positive attitude, throw out the negative in every area of your life, including media, as it detracts from your image and new life.

Nobody wants to hear about your problems.

In American culture, we greet people by asking, "How are you doing?" Please note this greeting is not an opportunity to disclose your laundry list of life problems caused by being a divorcee, widower, or widower. In the dating world, there is an excessive need to discuss the wrongs in one's life by delving into one's past. Too much negative information can kill a budding relationship before it begins.

The potential "Date" hears problems, problems, problems. They consider the weight of your baggage and wonder if they want to be involved. Some information is fine but there is a line as to how much one wants to hear about your past. *Remember you are trying to move forward in your life.*

Learn your wants, needs, and desires.
Don't give others the power to interfere
with your relationships too early.
Your children and family
will adjust to the new you.

Your new life is a canvas for *your* wants, needs, and desires. It's a chance to rediscover who you are, free from the constraints of past relationships and family responsibilities. For example, the last time you were alone may have been in your twenties, followed by raising your family, and a life centered around children, schools, and churches. Now, it's time to paint a new picture.

Discovering the "real you" takes work. Your earlier life was based upon compromise, relationship personalities, and concessions that may or may not have been a good fit for you. For example, you may have left behind passions such as tennis, horseback riding, hiking, girls' night outs, or book clubs to facilitate relationships and family.

Some of these changes may have been for the benefit of the family or the health of your significant other. Instead, you might have followed your partner's love of drag racing, car shows, and his friends, but now your life is all about "you." Your old friends might not fit into your new life because of your wife's or husband's involvement. Friendships change when you take a new path in life.

Now that you are single, you no longer feel comfortable limiting your social life to your group of married couples. Your interests are different, and you must grow into a new life. Whether you think new activities are fun or not, participate in them anyway. Explore many options, such as football, visiting historical places, pickleball, jogging, bicycle riding, bridge, horseback riding, book club, and hundreds of other opportunities.

Over time, you will find people with similar interests and, eventually, a dating or love interest. Life is so much more exciting when we, as a couple can find mutual interests.

Get to know other male and female friends and find relationships to build upon one another. During my darkest days, I served as a dinner greeter for families of critically ill members in the hospital. Volunteering at a hospital gave me a place to love and care for others as I kept myself busy. The hospital allowed me to serve and feel love. At that point, I needed to be hugged and held.

My volunteer activities provided an outlet to gain healthy affection versus embracing unknown men in bars. Get involved in your community, marketing groups, the American Red Cross, and churches. Your current social life does not need to be your passion but an avenue for future development to find people in similar situations. These activities give you a break from thinking about your problems and slow down the negative messages in your brain.

Life is not all about the guy or gal you will date but about the friends that you make along your single journey.

I found other creative ways to meet singles, with some approaches working better than others. I wanted to meet a like-minded man, so I went to church and stood in the back of the sanctuary until most people were seated. Then, I chose my seat next to a good-looking single man. Sounds silly, as I had no way of knowing if he was single, but no women were seated beside him. I'm unsure if this approach works, as the sample size was too small, and there was only one church.

Do not isolate yourself.

Do not compare your deceased spouse to your new relationship. In order to create a new relationship, you will need to make your home about you. Making your home about you is less intimidating to new friends.

In time, you will be ready to remove or relocate your departed spouse's treasures from common areas of your home. Part of your healing process is to remove his or her clothing. Work towards making your house "your home" with your tastes and accolades. It is unfair, callous, and rude for a potential mate to walk into your home with monuments of your departed on display. The memories from the past make the new relationship seem unimportant. Don't make your new mate be a caretaker for another's memory.

Maybe you are still awakening in the middle of the night to wander to the bathroom in the dark to not wake your significant other or avoid washing laundry at night for another's sake. Do you sleep in the bed facing the door because you are afraid? These behaviors are normal, and you can only cope with so much change in a given time. Learn to take every day on its merit and, in tough times, live moment by moment.

Give Yourself a Break!

Chapter 6

Self-Assessment

Assessment & Improvement Indicator

I HAVE BEEN in a situation similar to yours. While everyone's struggles are unique, having benchmarks of our former life helps us stay focused and motivated about the future. We can get past this emotional and financial jungle to find a new direction. By using the assessment tool every six months, you can determine progress. Your first assessment is where you plant your flag between your responsibilities, obligations, and the health of the old and new life.

Let's embark on a journey of self-discovery, a powerful tool to build a better life that is uniquely yours.
This process will empower you to take control of your life and shape your future.

You have been part of a couple that may not have represented your wants, needs, and interests. Now, you need to learn who "you" are individually. Being single changes everything in your life, and you need to develop your own identity as a single person. You must find someone compatible with your new lifestyle to find a successful new relationship. Throw away your feelings of inadequacy and let it all hang out (like the 70s songs). Just be you!

"Be The Prize!"

There is a tremendous rate of change in your life, so treat yourself with patience. Adjust your expectations and accept yourself. Healing a broken heart requires time, and timeframes are different for everyone. Healing takes as long as it takes.

You are surprised at how little the changes in your life affect you significantly, for example, leaving your home or living alone in the old house stresses you. The house now feels empty and quiet, undermining your feelings of stability.

After this chapter, I provide assessment tools so you can learn who you are today and retake these tests in six months. The trauma of ending an old life and finding a new life makes it hard to determine whether you are making progress and, if so, how much. Taking these tests regularly will help you determine areas that need work and measure your progress. Success motivates!

These tools can be both a barometer to help determine who you are and a key to interpret the compatibility of potential partners.

Airplanes have an altimeter to determine altitude. This navigation tool is especially important when pilots fly over large bodies of water. When the plane flies over the ocean, its reflection on the water makes it difficult to determine up from down. Not knowing where they are means crashing into the sea.

While we struggle in our single lives, it is difficult to determine if we are getting better or worse regarding our emotions, spiritual life, physical, financial, health, living arrangements, etc. This tool can help you periodically assess yourself and a potential mate. It is a line in the sand between our old and new life. It also aims to inspire you by determining improvement.

The following assessments determine where you are today: emotionally, psychologically, spiritually, sexually, financially, professionally, and the family's roles in your life.

They measure healthy and unhealthy habits. Copy the questions and retake every 6- 12 months to determine your progress.

For each question below, answer Yes or No and/or Rate Your Feelings on a scale of 1-10 (1 means you are not affected. 10 means you are significantly affected).

EMOTIONAL		Feelings 1-10	Yes/ No
	Sad/Depressed		
	Mentally		
	Happy		
	Stress Level		
	Confused		
	Nightmares		
	Negative Record Playing in Brain		
	Suicidal		
SPIRITUAL			
	Do you pray?		
	Do you spend time with a higher power?		
	Do you believe in God?		
	How much emotional support do you receive?		

PHYSICAL		Feelings 1-10	Yes/ No
	20 lbs + Overweight		
	Grey hair		
	Unkept Hair		
	Flexibilty		
	Fitness		
	Exercise Times per Week		
HEALTH			
	Quality of Health		
	Sexuality		
	Eat Fast Foods Times per Week		
	Diet Including Vegetables		
CAREER			
	Stability		
	No Job Underemployed		

FINANCES		Feelings 1-10	Yes/No
	Pay Bills on TIme		
	Supporting Two+ Households		
	Paying Daycare		
	Custody/Child Support		
	Spousal Support		
LIVING ARRANGEMENTS			
	Family Home		
	Apartment		
	Rental		
	Other (Fill In)		
LEVEL OF ATTRACTIVENESS			
	Wardrobe Up to Date		
	Hairstyle Up to Date		
	Hair Unkept		
	Midriff Tops/Overly Sexual		
	Lingerie or Granny Panties		
FINDING THE RIGHT PARTNER			
	Dating or Want to Date		
	Online Dating		
	Traditional Dating		

ALCOHOL/DRUGS		Feelings 1-10	Yes/No
	Alcohol Consumption		
	How Much Alcohol?		
	Drug Use		
	How Often?		
AGRESSIVENESS			
	Level of Agressiveness		
YOUR ROLES			
	Do You Have Children?		
	Live Away From Home		
	Live With You		
	Responsible for Adults (Like Parents)		
	Do They Live With You?		
	Ex Still in the Picture?		
	Own/Rent?Lease a Car		
	Interested in Another Mate?		
	Does Your Job Require Extensive Travel?		
	Do You Want to Date or Create a Relationship?		

ACTIVITIES and INTERESTS		Feelings 1-10	Yes/No
	Travel		
	Motercycles		
	Camping		
LIFESTYLE			
	Golf		
	Pickleball		
	Running		
	Walking		
	Board Games		
	Dancing		
	Other		
FAITH			
	Christian		
	Agnostic		
	Other		
PRIVATE TIME			
	How much do you have?		
	How much do you need?		

FLEXIBILITY		Feelings 1-10	Yes/No
	Spontaneous		
	Rigid		
	Curious		
	Playful		
TV and GAMES			
	Hours (Weekly) in Front of a Computer or TV		
	Hours (Weekly) Playing Games		
	Online		
	Virtual		
	Dancing		
SOCIAL			
	Family Only		
	Friends		
	Large Group		
ANIMALS			
	Dogs		
	Cats		
	Horses		
	Other		

Chapter 7

Confidence

Below is a letter from RM in Cambria, CA written to the author when he discovered his confidence.

"AFTER MY DIVORCE, I worked to establish myself as a single person. Then, I happened to meet Lynn. I am so glad I did. Lynn is open-minded, fun to talk to, and energetic. I feel open and free to talk about everything and mean everything, guys. Honest answers are made easy to grasp and apply.

We sorted through the online meeting sites and formulated ideas for presenting myself in a profile. Choosing the ladies to meet my desires and not wasting time on just a pretty face. She helped with engaging conversation and instructions on how to dress and NOT. Every time we talk, my questions are answered, and my confidence builds up. There are always new things to discuss, and Lynn has answers.

Here is one of the things I learned from Lynn. When you meet your date for the first time, in person or on a Zoom date, don't dress like you did when you divorced. Impress her with a collared shirt, casual pants, and shoes, like the man you are rebuilding, not what you were. You'll stand out from the other slobs. And don't come empty-handed.

A simple flower wrapped by a florist shows you are thinking and planning for your meeting. Your date will recognize the effort immediately. Trust me. When she sees you for the first time, and you stride up to her feeling confident, with a flower for the lady, she will like it, and so will you.

Good stuff, huh? This is me, Ron, 69 years old and ready to go after a 37-year marriage. Lynn has been a breath of fresh air for me from day one until today. I couldn't have done it without her. Working with Lynn is so valuable."

"Be the man you want to build. And don't show up for your first date empty-handed." RM

"Confidence is assurance, self-possession, aplomb meaning a state of mind, or a manner marked by easy coolness and freedom from uncertainty, diffidence, or embarrassment." (Merriam-Webster. Jan. 12, 2024).

Both success and failure produce confidence. Confidence and trust in your abilities come from studying and testing theories through research, modeling, repetition, and more. Developing an attitude of gratefulness feeds your feelings of confidence. But perhaps the most powerful tool in your arsenal is positive self-talk. This internal dialogue, supporting feelings of optimism and motivation, creates a constant source of encouragement.

Learn to dream as a child again. Remember your child-like curiosity, excitement, determination, love, and passion? Remember when you were flexible before lists of tasks took over your daily life? If you are going through trauma because of loss, you may have forgotten how to smile. At some point in time, you faked a smile by showing teeth in a grin, but the light in your eyes was gone. You've seen posed photos that show teeth without genuine joy. Find your smile again that exudes cheerfulness and take back your vitality. These behaviors contribute to your confidence.

Another powerful way to boost your confidence is by helping others. This act of altruism stimulates your attitude of gratitude but also allows you to share in other's successes. When you become another's cheerleader, your problems will seem smaller and less self-focused. My love of people, along with my past struggles, has made me confident. Now I can accomplish most things with enough preparation and repetition (except math!)

Trying extra activities can be a struggle, and you may look like a dork; however, when a noble cause helps others, it feeds you. Stay the course and you will not fail. Like we said in the sixties, "Let it all hang out." It's essential to recognize past situations, even the challenging ones, can be valuable learning experiences. Embracing these experiences can help you find the resilience and strength to overcome future challenges, fostering a sense of optimism.

When old problems and behaviors hold you back, it's crucial to identify them and face them straight on while building new skills. Self-reflection and growth empower you, making you feel more in control of your life. Lack of confidence and poor self-esteem pervasively affect your life, affecting work, school, and relationships. By listing your wins and losses, you learn from the past and use it as a springboard to propel you forward.

Confidence is attractive. Taking deep breaths, standing straight, sucking in your gut (even a 44" waist), squaring your shoulders, making eye contact, and keeping your chin up all project confidence. It engages and inspires trust. Improving your posture is as simple as exercising. You will find a few crunches improve your posture and aid in feeling better about yourself. Even just one set of ten crunches per day will improve your posture. Your goal will increase until you reach three sets of ten or a number you and your doctor agree upon. Think of how it feels to button your pants instead of just zipping them. Your stance improves, as will your self-esteem and sex appeal.

At an early age, I attended modeling school to prepare for queen contests. They taught me the value of eye contact and good posture. I gained confidence in presenting myself correctly: grooming, hair, makeup, and dressing to fit my body type. Preparation creates a greater awareness of the person you project and how others see you.

After being shown and with repetitive practice, I became very aware of my posture. Then I had a more confident way to meet the world and understood the importance of preparation. Remember the adage: "When you smile, the world smiles back at you." Consider all of your assets, including personality and accomplishments. You are so much more than you might credit yourself: You've successfully raised a family, met deadlines, and managed your time.

Having a career is not essential to your confidence. Remember, you wholeheartedly supported the schools, community activities, fairs, churches, etc. Everyone has value! Dig deep into your life for successes that inspire and create peacefulness. Good posture makes you look outwardly confident and self-assured. However, you must learn through repetition to achieve true confidence and peace.

Create a new habit of being good to yourself and stop negative self-talk like, "I always screw up" when nobody always does anything. There are things we do better and worse. Assess your life and behaviors for growth. We are a work in progress, so stop putting yourself down and learn to be your best friend.

**Create healthy habits,
increase confidence,
and stop negative behaviors.**

Confidence is helpful in a single life, as it can be hard to approach males or females in a social setting. There is a misconception that men must be Alpha males to be worthy of attracting and mating with a female. I have met many men who quit dating because they discovered they could never be an Alpha male. Some read books or listened to social media teaching them to be an Alpha. They learned to be insensitive to their partner, ignoring her opinions, wants, and needs. Their views and needs come first, regardless of their partner's wants, needs, or desires. Some women like this type of man, while others want to be respected.

I have tested the idea and found it wrong on many levels. Be the best and most authentic "you," and it will be good enough. My friends have found those teachings to be aggressive and not welcomed by many women. The men felt inadequate and unworthy of finding a woman to date, play, or procreate with.

Be aware of attractive and unattractive traits.

Nurture your healthy and attractive traits:

- Affectionate
- Caring
- Compassion
- Flexibility
- Forgiveness
- Humility
- Loving
- Loyalty

Work on the not-so-attractive traits:

- Anger
- Criticizing
- Domination
- Invasion of Privacy
- Isolation
- Rigidity
- Trespassing Over Boundaries
- Unforgiveness

Don't be afraid to show your sincerity and tenderness.

Chapter 8

Rule Your Life

THE FOLLOWING tips are for everyone creating new relationships and establishing boundaries. Below are examples of children taking advantage of parents and spouses as they age. These true stories affect men and women who marry or cohabitate. Those who create new long-term relationships may want to consider who will care for their mate and holdings when he or she dies. Though sad, these are all true stories.

Example #1: A couple has been married for 25+ years, and the wife dies. The wife's children and a construction crew arrive to remodel the house the following Monday. They told the grieving stepdad to find another place to live. The sounds of the 8 a.m. crew and the demolition waking him every day were unbearable. He was nearly 80 years of age, and suddenly, he was being pushed out of the home where he cared for his wife of twenty-five years.

There are two sides to every story, and this might not be illegal, but it is sad. There had to be a more caring way to handle that situation. Be aware.

He was forced away from his beautiful garden and serenity at a time when he was least able to cope with the loss of his lovely wife. His only choice was to move into a mobile home, as her daughters had taken over everything belonging to him and his wife, including personal items. The daughters never checked on their elderly stepdad, who had doted on their mom for years.

Example #2: A friend, Dan, and his wife had been married for 13 years, and he adored her. Dan's wife had died two months ago, he was despondent and not emotionally able to cope with her loss. Her daughters came and took over the house without any legal rights. Sure, he would eventually get the house back but he would have to rely on the court system to evict the stepdaughters. He was forced to rent a room to grieve until he could regain control of his home many months later.

Not knowing how to make his life work and still in a state of shock, he asked me to marry him during our first meeting. His want of marriage was not because I was special but because he wanted the pain of his lost love to go away. He touted lavish pensions, money, love, and care for me. He said that he would not live that much longer, and I would be set for life. This offer of marriage was not about me but him. He wanted to chase away the loneliness and fit another woman into his life so he could keep moving forward.

Surviving Spouse Displacement

I believe that surviving spouse displacement happens to more women than men. But whatever the case, these events occur when you are at the lowest point of your life. As an older person in the grieving process, you may not have the strength or health to advocate for yourself.

This subject was discussed in the Self-Assessment chapter, and due to the extreme consequences, I want to remind you to be mindful of children's relationships when seeking potential spouses. Will their children take care of you or take advantage as you advance in age? Yes, there are legal ways to manage that situation, but everyone thinks their kids are perfect and would never deprive their loved ones; according to my experience, that is overly-optimistic.

Take some guesswork out of determining which relationships are a good fit for you and your potential mate. Qualify your potential mates according to their opportunities and obligations to family and extended family, and determine what time and finances are left over for dating and long-term relationships.

Take inventory of your responsibilities, including your kids and their roles in your decision-making process. Include custody arrangements, decide when you are free to date, and which weekend mom or dad has the kids. Consider your travel requirements for business and when you pick up your children. Other responsibilities might include obligations to your elder parents' care and well-being. Now, consider the hours you work like a graveyard shift, your community activities, and other demands upon your time that are unique to you.

Are you obligated financially to adult children or in business with them? Now, take note of your potential mate's financial arrangements and obligations to kids and parents. You don't need to know this information on the first date, but very soon.

Choosing a Mate or Date?

Nobody wants to waste time with someone who will not fit into their lifestyle. For example, there is a wonderful man who is successful, creative, and crazy about his grandchildren. Nothing makes him happier than having sleepovers three times per week with his grandchildren.

He needs a woman who loves, enjoys children, and is completely unselfish with her time. This lifestyle issue needs to be considered when choosing a forever love. A woman wanting to travel the world and not be tied down may not be a good fit for this homebody. There is nothing wrong with either of them. Just be aware of the fit.

As we age, physical abilities, sports, and lifestyles can be one of the biggest barriers to new relationships.

It's important to resist the urge to change people once you've won their hearts, or worse, to change yourself to fit their expectations. Instead, strive to find a love who accepts you for who you are. As we age, it becomes increasingly difficult to make significant changes, so it's best to find someone who appreciates you as you are.

For singles over 50, it's important to know that grown children may view your finances as their future inheritance. They may not be comfortable with your change of lifestyle with a new relationship or long-term relationship. You spending money on luxury items or activities may threaten their inheritance. Your adult children probably won't be excited about the new partner in your life. They may see them as competition for your time, grandchildren, and future inheritance, regardless of their good intentions.

Understand that daughters and sons want to protect their parents. Girls don't give up their position as Dad's favorite gal easily. When qualifying a person for a date, I am very interested in information as to how much influence adult kids have over the man or woman's life. My children do not dictate my life, and I don't want someone else's kids to make my decisions. On the other hand, a good man or woman who cherishes their family might be a great fit.

I recently shared this situation with a dad who stated he was his own man and his son would never interfere with his decisions, financial or otherwise. Fast-forward a few months, and Dad has a new girlfriend who he is crazy about. They want to create a long-term relationship and hit the road to leave his sedentary lifestyle.

Dad took $5,000 out of the bank. His son called him the following day and asked what he was doing with the money. Dad then reminded the son he was the beneficiary on the bank accounts to make the inheritance process smooth and not for him to monitor.

Whose Life Is It, Anyway?

I know of a man who would not rock the boat or stand up to his children when they were disrespectful to his lady friend. The adult children would not be considerate of her time or feelings. She was a great lady and outstanding mate choice for a long-term relationship. Because of the lack of respect and consideration the lady broke off the relationship. Now he is lovelorn, eating and sleeping alone to appease his children, what a waste.

Kids don't understand their elders still need to be held, touched, and have a physical relationship until their last breath. I remember in my youth thinking people over 40 or 50 could not possibly have sex. I could not imagine how awful it would be to see someone older naked. I've changed my mind.

Many kids and families think they can fill the hole in your heart, but they cannot satisfy the part of you who needs to be your own person. We hunger for someone to hold us in the middle of the night, give us inspiration, and help us to carry our burdens.

Getting a new life will require flexibility for both you and your family. In the past you may have filled your time watching kids and grandkids. Maybe the family has gotten used to your not having a life and being constantly available for babysitting duties. Now you need to make time for yourself and new activities. The kids can get used to these changes, but it might take a while.

Introductions to Your Family

The first few times we fall in love, we're excited to introduce our new friend to the family. Presenting our new love too soon can be a big mistake. Introducing a new potential mate to young children can be confusing. Remember, they might be taking someone else's position in the family, such as mom, dad, or grandparent. The family may still be experiencing grief and need time to heal. While they want you to be happy, they are not ready or capable of sharing your joy immediately.

The younger children are confused about the third time you bring home a potential partner. They also want to give this person a name, like a new parent, nana, aunt, papa, or grandparent. I encourage you to consider putting off the love introduction until you can firm up your relationship. Adult family members with no modern dating experience may start counting your love interests.

Early in our dating life we are lonely and prone to fall in love with the first or second person who pays us attention. Initially, most daters want someone to save them from a life of living, sleeping, and growing old alone. Permit yourself to have your own life by not sharing too much with your children and grandchildren. You may be judged by what you share.

As a new couple, you must find a way to prioritize one another.

Create a life that allows you to captain your ship by not allowing others to infiltrate your relationship.

Others can introduce old problems that attacked your last relationship.

Chapter 9

Flirting

LET's explore the art of meeting new people, focusing on the respectful skill of flirting. This includes the subtle yet powerful tools of eye contact and smiles. The principles remain the same whether you've been out of the social scene for a while or are a seasoned flirt. While flirting with your spouse or significant other can be fun, the flirting we'll discuss here is about building new, respectful relationships.

Flirting with someone's man or woman in a committed relationship is not polite, and you would not want your husband or wife to witness this behavior. A big smile and eye contact make you look more attractive and show interest in a potential date. When we see a person we find appealing, we often light up. The better you are at this, the more romantic options you will create.

Some people seem to have the skill of "coming on to someone or flirting" naturally, while others can learn and improve. Flirting is a playful behavior showing romantic or sexual interest. Effective flirting involves verbal and nonverbal communication, but perhaps most importantly, it requires active listening. This skill is not just about showing genuine interest, but also about truly understanding and respecting the person you're flirting with.

Know your market when you flirt. A flirt or tease should consider the event and its formality, present company, or being one-on-one. Conversations must be appropriate to the surroundings, especially if someone might be listening in. Also, consider whether the receiver is uptight or relaxed.

Salespeople, food servers, and bartenders also engage in similar bantering or playful behavior. Great salespeople also use kidding or playing to romance customers for tips and sales, while others use a lot of wordplay like using words with multiple meanings.

The following is an authentic, funny story about sales, extreme friendliness, and the public. I worked for a well-known business at a huge event. I was in my 50s, shapely, and kind of pretty. These shows have uniform lines of commercial booths under vast tents. There was twelve feet of customer walking space, and salespeople on both sides of the aisle who worked the crowd aggressively as they passed through.

A man, 85 years old, comes by my booth and says that he cannot talk with me because his wife would think we were trying to date.

The tease, polite banter, and jokes associated with flirting are engaging. Your body language also speaks volumes. Your eye contact, smile, leaning closer, patting the hand of the person sitting next to you. Or, someone who deliberately brushes you with their hip while passing by. Flirtation may include a softer voice making the potential partner feel special. Remember, flirting is not just about showing interest; it's also about having fun and enjoying getting to know someone new.

Effective flirts observe the potential partner's likes, dislikes, hobbies, and more. This attentiveness shows you care about the person they are flirting with and helps them to connect on a deeper level. Some flirting examples are "I see that you have photographed Yosemite, my favorite place." "I like your views on raising dogs, and it would be nice to know you better." Study your potential date, question their interests, like sports, hobbies, horses, and photography, and **always be genuine.**

Remember, the key to successful flirting is not just about showing interest; it's about being authentic and respectful. Express your admiration or interest respectfully and genuinely, and you'll exude confidence and self-assurance, knowing you're being true to yourself.

Inappropriate flirting at the first meeting can sound like this, "You have a nice body, and I'd like to hold it against me." Or bragging about your anatomy. On the first date, this is inappropriate and sounds cheap depending on the audience; it makes people feel uncomfortable. When you already know the person, it might seem charming. Of course, adjustments are made on a case-by-case basis.

Timing is everything. If you have known someone for a long time, sexual or aggressive flirting may be accepted or ignored. However, if you have just met a woman and make a personal comment like, "I am attracted to women with big boobs." Her response might be to lose her number. Know your market, delivery, style, and sex appeal.

Insincerity, lack of respect, and desperation are disappointments. Desperation is when you have been talking to a man for thirty minutes at a nightclub, and suddenly, he says, "It is midnight. Come home with me tonight?"

There is a theory in the single community: "If I ask twenty-five women to go home with me tonight, one will." That might be true for some, as singles are a lonely bunch. This can sound like a dating player who wants to date a different woman and have casual, intimate dates every night. The story below is about a casual, intimate "player" who is hurt by a "lady player."

Sam is a lovely, friendly man who has been a superficial dating player with a new woman every night. When he turned 60, he decided he was ready to settle down. He began flirting with a beautiful lady for weeks. He invited her to meet at his home before going to an upscale restaurant.

His date, Susie, did not want to go anywhere as she arrived with Chinese food in hand. His thinking was this is a different type of date and ate dinner and played along. Susie's plans included satisfying more than her taste buds. She wanted to play with him and made that clear.

They played, and he invited her to a nice restaurant the following night. Again, she showed up at his house with dinner in hand, this time Italian food. Her motive was to spend another intimate evening with him. This dinner and intimate routine went on for months. He felt used and disappointed when she would not settle down with him.

In 2025, "Dating players" are not always men.

Not everyone who dates wants to create and grow a long-term relationship, although many do.

Chapter 10

Romance

IN THE EARLY 1970s, love and romance books became very popular. Books like *Sweet Savage Love* and the *Harlequin* book series became well-known. These books gave people exciting ideas about what romance was.

Some books were sweet and tender love stories—expressive, descriptive, seductive, and passionate. Back then, the readership was primarily women, but many men, including my 80-year-old uncle, read them.

Those books created images of a man built like a Greek God, handsome cowboy, or a mysterious millionaire, and traveling to foreign lands. Romance writing went like this: "He brushes her radiant red locks tenderly, as his fingers trail to her collarbone and then down to her heaving breast. She longs for him as she touches his body with her hungry arms. Fiery waves of passion rage through their bodies as they explore one another."

Some girls dream about Prince Charming picking them up on a noble white steed and living happily ever after. Romance books and wedding movies plant these notions.

This messaging may have increased women's expectations about romance, shaping romantic notions and providing validation. What romance means to individuals involves experiences, personality types, and the individuals themselves. Women's high expectations make it tough on men. Achieving these dreams is a big goal.

Flirting opens the door for romance including early gestures like showing interest. Keeping the romance alive in your relationships forever, keeping the fire going, makes for good fun. You can't out-give a giving partner. Romance creates a fresh level of excitement and passion that leads to intimacy.

Today, I was questioned, "Is the most romantic gesture leaving a note under your love interest's pillow?" It is a grand gesture, and yes, it is fun to be surprised by love notes. Finding a love note in my lunch, car, purse, or even written on the bathroom mirror would also be fun. The element of surprise is exciting. There is no one-size-fits-all response for women.

I connected with a man via an online dating site and we met for dinner. He brought small flowers in a vase that said, "In life, most people do big things, but it is life's small things that make a difference." This man had taken his time to analyze my profile, type the note into a ribbon, and tie it on the vase. It was a lovely, unforgettable gesture, and a shame we were not a good fit.

In my life, small things make the biggest difference. You can take a person who appears poorly groomed to a $500.00 dinner and it sends the message this date is unimportant. The general mood and attitude of your date are essential. For example, you are eating dinner and find the entire focus of the conversation as being based upon sex. Or a date with an octopus. When the complete focus is on intimacy, it is a turnoff. I have walked out of dates and demanded no future contact be made.

I have discussed this situation openly and have been asked, "What kind of guys do you date who act so sexual?" My dates have included non-professional and professionals where most men were gentlemen. You might think this is a low-class problem, but sometimes men with money or power feel deserving of having their desires fulfilled, so there is no distinction between socioeconomic classes. The person they portray in public can be very different than a one-on-one in private with the opposite sex.

I love and appreciate old-fashioned gentlemen. Being romanced by opening the door, bringing flowers, leaving love notes, sending a song in the middle of the day, cuddling, and satisfying our need to be held. Listen for the heart's unspoken words and nuisances unique to one another saying, "You get me."

The gentle stroke of the cheek calms the mind and quietly reassures they are on my team. Sweet, comforting words are music to our ears, chase away fears, and remind us that we are not alone. We long for someone who offers a shoulder to lean on.

These gestures, big or small, are not just acts of kindness but expressions of caring and appreciation. Given compatibility, nothing leads to a physical relationship faster than genuine interest, flirting, and caring. Especially when one places the other person's needs above their own.

Romance is exciting and playful behavior boosting our morale, leading to future intimacy!

Enjoy!!

Chapter 11

Intimacy

INTIMACY CONSISTS of close personal connections, emotional and physical, requiring a certain amount of vulnerability that can be frightening. It's about connecting at a deeper level. When someone gets close to us, our confidentiality is threatened, and we may feel as though we are losing control of our lives.

When this person sees my inside information, will they use the knowledge to judge me if the relationship fails? And then there is the internal conversation: Does he or she like me as much as I like them? Or the other question: What happens if he quits loving me, and can my heart stand the loss?

Fear of rejection is real and overwhelming for both men and women. You may even feel emotionally unstable as you try to text or contact the potential partner too often. Trust is a big issue, and over-communication brings forth a sense of distrust or baggage. Setting boundaries gives a sense of control, and it is good advice to take the relationship slowly. Yeah, right!

I studied hundreds of men and women, asking them, "What words and expressions say intimacy to you?" While the order varied, the following words were used repeatedly: touch, encouragement, thoughtfulness, open communication, sharing likes and dislikes (public and personal), warmth, friendliness, responsiveness, empathy, confidentiality, authenticity, vulnerability, honesty, and truthfulness.

Open communication, confidentiality, and thoughtfulness emerged as the most valued expressions of intimacy. Words of encouragement and affirmation are compelling. Those words make even the most challenging days brighter and foster a sense of teamwork and mutual support in a relationship.

Intimacy, romance, and sex are distinct yet interconnected aspects of relationships. These behaviors and feelings have a unique role in relationships and dating activities. In my survey, the women revealed a lack of romance and intimacy in today's dating scene.

However, some men stated they were afraid to open doors and offer considerate gestures for fear of being misunderstood. A generation ago, gentlemen's behaviors included opening doors. In today's political environment, doing something a woman can accomplish by herself can be mistaken as sexism. She can open the door, so she does not need a man's help. These new behaviors in the past would have been considered courteous but can be grounds for reprimand in today's workplace. The new rules regarding courtesy are blurred. And how does the man win?

Think of a man in a position of authority, like a manager, owner, or corporate president. He has dozens of female employees. Opening doors, picking up dropped items, or speaking familiarly can be seen as favoritism, flirting, or the receiver owing a favor later.

The following dating situation could have been romantic if we had known one another. This scenario is a case of too much too soon. Timing is everything. A gentleman named Sam worked very hard to impress me. He treated me like a lady. Sam went over the top on the first date with many romantic gestures. He brought flowers from his garden and planned a lovely dinner with salmon and trimmings.

After dinner, there came the cake—a special cake, one with giant sparklers. The sparks jumped a foot into the air. I was in stimulation overload as I gazed at the flaming cake before me. He had purchased a Special Romantic Package for our first date, so he tried to pull me in for a kiss to be photographed. I was so confused.

These gestures put extra pressure on our date: meeting, eating, and kissing in front of a camera within a few hours. As he drove away, he reminded me that he found me physically attractive. "He liked my body, and we should date soon."

Despite trying too hard for the first date, he was a lovely man, but he caught me completely by surprise. He deserved a medal for putting himself out there with courage and without fear of rejection. I hope I represented him well. Due to his effort, he should have been King for a Day! A woman would love that kind of treatment in an established relationship.

Ignite her passion before going over the top.

Both intimacy and romance are part of the mating dance, but you can't rush it.

There is an order to creating a relationship.

Chapter 12

Mating Games

MY EDUCATION and career have been based on cultivating people, creating relationships, working teams, and growing businesses. When designing businesses and fitting employees, you must consider the required tasks, personality types, and learning styles to create the best work teams. For this book, we will use the stereotype indicators of Alpha and Beta in the dating world because of their simplicity and name recognition.

The Meyers-Briggs Type Indicator (MBTI) would be a standard theory for in-depth personality predictors in business. My goal is to show that all people are valuable and have strengths and weaknesses. Become aware of individual characteristics.

The terms Alpha and Beta originally came from the studies of wolves, with the leader becoming known as the Alpha and the followers being Beta. People are more complicated than wolves, but some of these ideas have been adapted to the dating world. (Calm.com, November 19,2024)

Leaders possess a set of traits and followers possess other traits that complement the team. Those traits vary in degree according to the expertise and tasks at hand.

For example, a team composed of all Alpha leaders is one of ideas and visionaries. Daily implementation and production require a distinct set of skills and personality strengths. Betas are a good choice as they would be someone who does not need the spotlight, can feel satisfied, and possess patience for more tedious tasks.

Alpha, Beta & Dating

Alpha traits include the desire to be in charge, are often charming, confident, curious, and are visionaries with leadership skills. In the dating world, the Alpha tends to attract more women. They are like the shiny objects in the pond: highly visible, often living "out loud" and comfortable with onlookers' attention. They are more assertive, and exude the confidence to directly approach a person of interest.

The downside of Alpha's personality can lack patience, be aggressive, and need control. They may dominate the decision-making process. Their jobs may include sales, entrepreneurs, heads of companies, and those who blaze their own paths.

The Beta male is gentle, reserved, selfless, loyal, collaborative, and a Mr. Nice Guy. He enjoys emotional connection, harmony, and being passive and cooperative. They enjoy living lives out of the limelight and working in the field or a quiet office.

Beta personalities avoid controversy, decision-making, and competition. Not always standing up for themselves or their opinions, nor taking charge, or communicating. But because Betas are not necessarily leaders, that does not mean they cannot lead.

I've heard Beta men in the dating world say to me, had I not come up to them, they would not have been bold enough to seek my attention. Betas tend to gravitate to careers that help people in the community, like doctors and nurses.

Alpha and Beta usually possess traits in both categories and exist in women as well. People are made up of many traits that can be situational. One might exhibit different leader or follower traits based on expertise. You may be a leader in nuclear science but not in psychology, as you are content to listen and take a quieter role.

Alpha has perceived advantages in the dating world in attracting more potential mates. Let's break down some traits that make Alpha special or different in dating. Alpha traits include confidence, great grooming, ambition, curiosity, competitiveness, self-reliance, and comfort in most social environments. Beta males are more patient in the decision-making process. They tend to be supportive and collaborative.

As a woman, I possess many good and bad Alpha traits. I love my ideas and people, am endlessly curious, and prioritize good grooming. I am driven and passionate about most things that I do. True to Alpha characteristics, I often lead and can be short on patience. Especially when I don't think issues are dealt with promptly.

In contrast, I don't want to be the leader at home or in romance. But I want to be a teammate and not always wait for the man to care for me. Or I am perceived as very able and not needing a man. It is a paradox, and I am sharing it to show you how easily a power struggle can develop between two Alpha types. I have been attracted to Alpha, but it has seldom met my needs when we have had the same Alpha downsides, like the lack of patience.

For some women, tight boundaries create feelings of security. Learn your partner's needs and communicate. Some women enjoy having someone who takes care of all the details as opposed to a team approach.

I recognize the strengths and weaknesses of both the Alpha and the Beta. Now I appreciate Beta's qualities like being non-confrontational, sensitive, and considering the needs of others. As women, we need to be open-minded to Beta qualities while seeking a mate.

Communicate, Communicate, and Create Genuine Friendships!!

The pressure on men to conform to Alpha ideals is often unjust. Some teachers and media encourage men to become Alpha vs. Beta to increase the number of dates or relationship opportunities they achieve. They also encourage them to dismiss women's conversations regarding their wants, needs, and desires. These men are led to believe that they know better, as women cannot understand their minds.

I have witnessed the emotional struggle of men who have strived to embody Alpha traits to attract more women. Ironically, they learned these behaviors from men who seemed oblivious to women's perspectives. My male friends, who were the Beta type, were naturally gentler and more selfless. After reading many singles books, they felt the pressure to conform to the Alpha idea. They believed only Alpha males were deemed worthy of successful females.

Their studies encouraged them to be aggressive and controlling, teaching them dominance was the key to winning over women. For those men, their studies backfired, leaving them feeling like failures unworthy of female companionship. In their misguided attempts to conform to the Alpha ideal, they became more arrogant and controlling, losing their gentleness, transparency, and authenticity.

This behavior does not foster healthy relationships. Ultimately, couples must function as a team, communicative and free from overly controlling behaviors that diminish compatibility. Yes, these traits may benefit a ruler or a winner, but winners and losers do not create harmony in a home or relationship.

I believe there is a head of the household, but that person is only successful if both parties are included in the decision-making process. The other person should not be relegated to suffer the consequences without a voice. The buck must stop somewhere.

Dating Communication

Men must listen to women's cues, both verbal and nonverbal, when coaxing and schmoozing her into sexual submission. Manipulation to engage in sex without communication can seem empty. Women are not conquests equaling a man's wins or losses based upon the seduction successes.

Some men in my study quit dating because they could not possess the traits of the dominant Alpha personality and felt unworthy of mating. Another incorporated the narcissistic idea that men must show women who are the boss by demanding his will over hers.

Taking Advantage:
Relationship and Sexual Games

I love men but can't believe that some will adopt predatory behaviors for their dating entertainment, but this is true. Below are some dating games I have witnessed.

Game #1: Begins by the male asking twenty-five ladies sitting in a bar to go home with them, and one woman will. I questioned these men, and their successes based on their return to the bar week after week as they continued to play the same game. They commented that this method of taking home a woman every night works. Younger men seem more attracted to this game, as it is another notch in their belt.

Game #2: Begins with two men seeking an older woman to buy her drinks until she is inebriated. The idea is to take a drunk woman home once she has lost her ability to drive safely. I witnessed these behaviors and did not know how her night went after she left the bar with the help of two strangers. More explanation, I do not judge her, as I understand our singles' loneliness. One can be easily swayed to make poor decisions, especially with the help of alcohol.

Never, Never, Never Lose Control Over Yourself When Out With Others.

Both single women and men want companionship and/or sex, with some wanting sex sooner than others. Whether Alpha or Beta, there is plenty of room for nice guys and girls who want mutual caring, love, and respect. Many women appreciate the transparency of a man who is strong enough to share his vulnerabilities. You do not need to train yourself to be something you are not to find love.

Yes, to Self-Improvement

Congratulations on the self-improvement that makes you the best "you." Learning skills like confidence will help with assertiveness, improved communication, and authenticity. We have heard the story about not throwing the baby out with bathwater.

Don't throw away what is
Good within yourself to become the unknown.

Guard your unique qualities.

You don't have to be someone else to be loved
But being polished helps!

A combination of Alpha and Beta traits has its place in our lives and society. Corporations and individuals alike have learned combined personality traits build better and stronger relationships and productive work teams.

Society needs leaders and followers. In the end, we want relationships with people who are good, cooperative, sensitive, and kind. Isolate his or her qualities and traits you perceive as negative. Embrace the qualities and work to improve the negative traits.

Improving your grooming is a priority. Good grooming is attractive and gives confidence when you enter the room. Whereas poor grooming separates people into different social and economic worlds. It is not about the money, but about your presentation. Don't say this is how I am, and he or she needs to understand I don't enjoy grooming. That's true, but you also don't enjoy being alone, sleeping alone, eating alone, etc.

Work on your confidence by getting involved with people, your hobbies, and charities. Find your joy regardless of personality type. While some find joy by hiking and playing sports, my joy and happiness comes from helping others. A joyful person attracts people, where a grump drives them away.

For an example of dating/mating games I've experienced, check out My Dating Stories, in Bonus Chapter #19.

Chapter 13

Menopause

This is my story of Menopause, which is meant to increase attention to your body's big transition into menopause. I am allowing you to look at my pain during the early years of menopause and hope to increase your attentiveness to your body or hers. I am not saying your transition through menopause will be as eventful as mine, nor typical of yours or others. I am saying be observant and good to yourself. Life is short, and this situation will not get better on its own.

From a woman who was struck down unnecessarily in her prime and took ten years to recover.

I am not a doctor or a therapist, these are my truths.

AT ONE TIME, I was a vibrant banker and the mother of a small child. Suddenly, I needed a hysterectomy caused by endometriosis and a mass. I had the surgery and expected to recover in six to twelve weeks and be as good as new. The doctor said, "I left the playpen, enjoy."

Within months of the surgery, I began having sleep difficulties and my memory was foggy. And like a thief in the night, my health and well-being were undermined. My body was overheated, and while the refrigeration was turned to the lowest setting, I was freezing my family despite their electric blankets. Then came a series of seemingly unrelated symptoms.

The following year I exhibited more arbitrary symptoms. And the local doctors chased one pain at a time and could not yet see the condition. Body pain, monthly infections, flu-like symptoms, then damage to my right eye, facial paralysis, very little reflexes on my right side and weaknesses that would not allow me to walk more than 50 feet. As a past athlete and horseman, I could not comprehend my diminished mobility. I could no longer work.

My former internist had retired, so nobody in the medical community knew me. The new doctors treated me like I was looking for an easy way out of the work world.

Sex became unattainable, and the daily pain in the pelvis and bladder was unbearable. I went to a local doctor to discuss the pain during intercourse, and he said,

"Don't let your husband be so rough and demand gentleness."

My husband was never abusive. Go to the doctor or don't go to the doctor, I was still struggling alone. The treatment I got from the local doctor was like emotional sabotage, staying home and praying for a better tomorrow was less frustrating. And I did it day after day, month after month, year after year.

I was 33 years old, making no progress, and had lost confidence in local doctors. We decided to travel to the Stanford Medical Center for another opinion. When I arrived at the Stanford Medical Center, I had no stamina, and the six-hour round trip in a day was too much for me to endure. Going to the medical center required a driver and an overnight stay in a hotel. After running a battery test, the doctors at Stanford stated I needed more than four times the amount of estrogen prescribed locally.

The doctors at the Stanford University Medical Center stated I had been administered an incorrect dosage of estrogen. The low dosage of hormones caused my vagina to atrophy, making sex nearly impossible and the pain unimaginable. Penetration felt as though my body was split in half. The lack of estrogen also caused pelvic pain and bladder issues.

By that time, the doctors diagnosed me with chronic fatigue syndrome, a possible stroke that damaged my right eye, facial paralysis, and reduced reflexes on my right side. They determined I also had a sleep issue that later became known as Sleep Apnea.

Doctors at Stanford Medical Center and the Social Security Administration determined that due to my deteriorated condition, they did not expect me to regain my health. As a result, they put me on permanent Social Security Disability.

My diagnosis could have been found in my hometown through a simple blood test. But like most young people, I did not have a doctor-patient relationship locally. Doctors did not trust my words of pain and sickness because I had a small child. It seemed that the doctors stereotyped me, thinking I wanted to be a stay-at-home mom. As a result, doctors had not observed my decline, and that, coupled with the fact that I had a small child, meant I wanted to stay home. Locally my symptoms were not taken seriously by my doctor, although family, friends and church knew differently.

After a length of time suffering through a variety of illnesses, the people from my church were very concerned and involved in my daily care, including transporting my daughter to and from school. By then, I could scarcely get out of bed. My family and extended family picked up our groceries.

I had been the church community events chairman, but was too ill to attend or participate in the annual event that attracted 1,500 people. My illness prevented me from attending, so I made cakes for the church to sell or use for the cakewalk. The drastic change in my health left people concerned they would risk their health if they consumed cakes. Nobody bought or consumed any of the dozen cakes for fear that my illness could be passed on to them. Shortly after the church event, many of the congregation came to say their "goodbyes."

After spending years as an outpatient at Stanford University Medical Center and years of healing against all odds, I won. Becoming healthy was job one, and I returned to school to learn how to read and write again. Returning to health took ten years for recovery. There were many challenges, but now I am able-bodied!

Thank you, Jesus!

I am here, I am proof, I am Lynn!!!

I can do all things through Christ who strengthens me! (Phil. 4:13)

The silver lining of my illness was my daughter learned empathy and how to physically take care of another person at a young age. As a result, our family and society benefited when she became a school nurse. Had I not gotten sick, I probably would not have known her because I was a workaholic.

Menopause and Symptoms

Menopause is a significant transition that women usually begin between 45 and 55 years of age. The transition occurs naturally; however, in my case, it happened suddenly at the age of 33. These physical and physiological changes started abruptly, as there were no ovaries or uterus and, therefore, no menstrual cycle. Eventually, all women go through menopause if they live long enough.

I had all the symptoms below:

Hot flashes

Sleep Interruptions

Moodiness

Bladder Control

Vaginal Dryness

Missed Menstrual Cycles

Weigh Gain

Body Mass

Muscle Loss

Depressive symptoms

Energy & Metabolism

Change in Sexual Function

My symptoms may not be all-inclusive.
For accurate and up-to-date information for yourself, visit the National Institute of Health, Cleveland Clinic, or Mayo Clinic online.

Hormone Therapy & Potential Benefits

Some time passed, and once I had the correct amount of estrogen, I got relief from hot flashes, night sweats, vaginal dryness, and relief of painful intercourse. Sex became more comfortable and my libido improved. However, the recurrent history of bacterial infections and yeast prevailed.

A common complaint for women after a hysterectomy, or as we age, is the need for lubrication. There is an assortment of lubricants, ranging from oil-based to silicone bases. My doctor also recommended coconut oil, and since then, I have used almond oil, aloe vera, and commercial lubes. To the wise, consider the thickness of the oils and lubes you use. Some of the oils will run out of your hands like water, and be a little messy, making some oils hard to catch...HA!

My goal for this chapter is to help both males and females come to terms with this new reality of menopause, whether it be a hysterectomy, the natural progression, or through chemo.

As I write this portion of the book, I feel conflicted about sharing too much and being too personal. I questioned myself, "How can I help others if I am unwilling to be transparent?" If you are going through menopause the way that I did, you might be encouraged by someone who traveled your path. I emerged after 10 years of recovery and learned to read and write again. I am as good as new. Again, my lengthy recovery is not typical, so do not fear the menopause process when it comes to you.

I have a love and passion for making sure our voices are heard.

For the men reading this, I ask for your empathy. I encourage you to go to doctor's appointments with her. While she is going through menopause, she may not be herself (emotionally, physically, or mentally), and may not get the treatment or attention she deserves without your help and understanding.

I don't want to scare you from lifesaving treatment.

It's not as though you have a choice to go through menopause or not!

Chapter 14

Erectile Dysfunction (ED)

A Hurdle <u>Not</u> a Barrier

This chapter is included at the request of men who struggle physically and emotionally with Erectile Dysfunction (ED).

My ED panel named the erectile dysfunction chapter "A Hurdle, <u>Not</u> a Barrier."

As a thank you to the men and women who supported my research, I am dedicating this chapter to them.

I encourage men to reach out to their physician and therapist; don't suffer in silence.

THE MEN INCLUDED in this study had already been diagnosed with Erectile Dysfunction (ED) by doctors and therapists. They agree that this information should be more accessible, mainstream, and open for discussion in a more readable format. These men are from all walks of life and professions. My goal is to give a voice to them and their partners who are also affected. This encourages men who fight the embarrassment and isolation and seek treatment. In addition, I want to supply resources for you to investigate.

True story: one of the first statements of a newly single man over 50 is, "I am not sure if my body still works." After a long period of little or no sex, he was stressed over the idea of nonperformance. Sexual issues can start in the twenties, but most symptoms usually start later in life.

A common scenario involves a man who is over fifty and has spent the past ten years sleeping in the second bedroom. The man states that his body works fine for self-satisfaction, but he fears the loss of performance ability in a romantic setting. He remarks that self-satisfaction requires only a few minutes, but tender interludes with a partner take longer, and there lies one of the reasons men worry.

Help is out there. There are government sites like the National Institute of Health with up-to-date articles by SW Leslie (who cites 177) with information regarding identification and treatments. As you become more informed, perhaps you can find hope and peace.

My experience, research, as well as professional relationships with those affected provide a nonjudgmental look at the inside of sex, ED, and relationships.

What are the Symptoms of ED?

According to the National Institute of Health, symptoms of ED include the inability to:

- Get an erection sometimes, but not every time you want to
- Get an erection, but do not have it last long enough for sex
- Get an erection at any time

https://www.niddk.nih.gov/health-information/urologic-diseases/erectile-dysfunction/symptoms-causes

"There are many factors that can cause the vascular, nervous, and endocrine systems to cause or contribute to ED." (NIHDK, 04/02/24)

Diseases and Conditions That Can Lead to ED

- Type 2 /Diabetes
- Heart & blood vessel disease (NIH)
- Atherosclerosis
- High blood pressure
- Chronic kidney disease
- Multiple sclerosis (NIH)
- Peyronie's disease

Injuries from treatments for or to:

- Prostate cancer (NIH), including radiation therapy and prostate surgery
- The penis, spinal cord, prostate, bladder, or pelvis
- Bladder cancer surgery (NIH)

Men who have diabetes are two to three times more likely to develop ED than men who do not. Read more about diabetes and sexual and urologic problems at **The National Institute of Health, NIH)**

Certain medications have ED as a side effect, including:

- Blood pressure medicines (NIH)
- Medicines for prostate cancer therapy (NIH)
- Antidepressants (NIH)
- Tranquilizers or prescription sedatives
- Appetite suppressants, or drugs that make you less hungry
- Ulcer medicines

Certain health-related factors and behaviors that may contribute to ED

- Smoking
- Drinking too much alcohol
- Using illegal drugs

- Being overweight
- Not being physically active

As per (niddk.nih.gov), the recommendation is to undergo medical tests with a urologist, as well as mental health and physical exams.

Another great website: https://healthcare.utah.edu/mens-health/conditions/erectile-dysfunction/trimix-injection

Lots of ED prescription medicines are taken orally, except Trimix, which is injectable (from the NIH website)

- Sildenafil (Viagra)
- Vardenafil (Levitra, Staxyn)
- Tadalafil (Cialis)
- Avanafil (Stendra)
- Alprostadil, Papaverine, and Phentolamine: injectable (TriMix)

NIDDKI scientist and other experts: Tom Lue, M.d. University of California San Francisco. Email to healthinf@niddk.nih.gov

Attitude and communication are essential between a couple experiencing Erectile Dysfunction, as well as the need to put embarrassment aside. The cycle of dealing with ED progresses something like this: both partners want to be held, kiss and loved. The prelude to sex involves touching, holding, and caressing. At some point, the excitement and desire for sexual intercourse and penetration occurs. Or does it?

All the while, in the moments leading up to the sexual encounter, the man is determined, anxious, and afraid that he cannot complete the task but bravely tries anyway. His sexual disappointment during the relationship can crush his feelings of manhood and affect many other areas of his life. The frustration from the bedroom can be seen outside of the bedroom and exhibited through anger and withdrawal. As women, we need to recognize and help overcome frustration.

Erectile Dysfunction Affects Her, Too.

Sex is a team sport, and those intimate moments can go like the following:

1. The loving couple is caressing, and the man's attempts to penetrate are incomplete. His devastation is felt by both he and the woman who tries to help him recover his self-worth (to make the man feel better about himself). This repeated process takes the 'team' out of the team sport, thus making the interlude all about him.

2. She makes herself available for him when he is ready, even though she is not. She may increase her efforts at holding, caressing, touching, and playing. As this process repeats itself over and over, it can become about helping a man retain his dignity and less about her.

You can take the same situation when the man experiences a different attitude, one when he forgives himself and accepts his physical limitations. He keeps trying. One couple stated that 'team' masturbation and sometimes the act of watching a partner get excited has been known to work well for them.

I know of people who lost their relationships due to ED when a fresh approach may have saved the day. The frustration often drives one party or the other away. He removes himself in times of emotional or physical challenges. As a result, shutting the other person out.

Men bring the sexual party.
Does it have to be that way?

Most men grew up believing the success of the physical relationship depended solely on them. Their performance has taken on the burden of making the physical relationship, aka sexual satisfaction, their responsibility. That was possibly accurate and easy in your youth and prime.

However, intimacy changes over the years, requiring creativity, understanding, and emotional openness to help. Our bodies change, as does the need to become flexible and accepting. Learn to enjoy the physical journey, live in the moment, and love every touch.

If your goal is purely to reach orgasm, you will find *disappointment*. Learn to enjoy sexual journeys. Contrary to what many people think, you can have a very loving relationship without penetration. There's the holding, caressing, touching, and toys. There are toys for him and some for her.

Toys come in different sizes and shapes; some vibrate, while others do not. There are toys for the penetration of multiple locations: vaginal, oral, and anal. Included within their inventory are lotions, condoms, bras, seductive costumes, and t-shirts. Most stores have knowledgeable and helpful staff to guide you.

These toys can be bought online and delivered in brown, non-descriptive packages. Most of your larger cities have adult stores that sell toys and seductive clothing. Going into adult stores can be intimidating, and you may have the urge to hide your car, so nobody knows you are inside. You're there for the same purpose if you encounter someone you know. For those who are intimated by the physical location, you are best served by using an online adult store.

ED and Dating

Dating men don't want to be embarrassed in person and will often share their ED status before meeting via phone, text, or on their first date. I feel that if you are a man who is dating someone close to your age, most women will understand; however, if you are dating women in their 30s, you may have to educate them on the challenges of ED.

I have seen men experience the highs and lows of trying to remain sexual while affected by erectile dysfunction. I want to be your motivator and encourage both men and women to continue to work through the ED process.

You only lose if you quit trying!

Spice up your relationship by improving communication and being open to toys, role-playing, or whatever brings enjoyment to you as a couple.

I also suggest some professional tools and references from multiple sites, which are found at the end of this book. I am not a doctor, just a gal who has lived the experience from a different point of view and lots of research.

As you can see, I am addressing both men and women affected by the ED. You need to be reminded that sex is a team sport, and the overall health of the relationship depends upon meeting one another's needs. It is not to be solely based on man's attempts, successes, or failures.

While men have their challenges with their bodies, women also have their obstacles. Menopause and its symptoms, such as dryness, pain, and hormonal difficulties, are frustrating to women as well. Learn to enjoy the journey. Keep holding and touching because the health of your relationship depends upon it. Sex is a team endeavor.

Chapter 15

Alcohol and Drugs

THIS CHAPTER IS about alcohol involvement in a single person's life. Alcohol is what we dump on problems when they are already insurmountable. Many consume alcohol to drown out misery and find sleep when peace is nowhere to be found.

My goal is to remind you of the cost and unpredictability of alcohol in our lives. I'm sharing the story of "Sam," a good friend whose wife had died. Before her death, they only consumed wine on special occasions. They had a great marriage, one that most will dream of.

After her death, he started drinking at home regularly and then drank his way around town to multiple bars. Soon he could not go home to his quiet house until he was stumbling drunk. Others and I tried to help but to no avail. My friend "Sam" died alone in 2024, after many attempts to save him from alcoholism and hopelessness.

Sam was handsome, looked much younger than his age, and possessed every comfort money could buy. He had every attribute a women could want and he longed for a woman's companionship. However fine ladies were not interested in the drunk he had become. He could not stay away from the alcohol.

Maybe you've never drank to excess, but the instability of a single life makes one ripe for alcohol abuse. Everyone who drinks does not have alcoholism, but some are genetically prone. First, a glass or two of wine sneaks into our single lives. Later, it takes the place of families, close relationships, jobs, health, and everything that we hold dear.

Alcohol and Living Single

In the American culture, offering a visiting guest something to drink is polite. As you visit single friends, you are typically provided with a drink and often alcohol. Consider how you might visit multiple friends several times per week and date occasionally. Now, you can easily indulge in drinking alcohol nearly every night without a second thought.

Alcohol is Everywhere in the Single World

Entertainment venues are everywhere, from bars to wineries and even movie theaters. Wineries are some of the most successful local attractions for singles as they feature great musical talent and Las Vegas-quality shows.

As a spectator, tailgating at sporting games and sports bars includes a lot of alcohol.

Churches and other non-alcohol groups are working hard to attract the same singles but with a lesser success rate. As a result, finding venues for singles in a non-alcoholic world is challenging.

Actively participating in physical sports is a good way to improve your fitness, meet people, and avoid the alcohol crowds. I acknowledge that spectator sports like football integrate alcohol. Be active, get involved with life, and meet with others with similar interests. Maintaining an active body helps create a peaceful mind by burning off excessive energy.

Spectator sports are exciting, passionate, and high energy. Alcohol and watching sports doesn't make us physically tired nor does it quiet our busy minds and help us find peace. The alcohol connections are on a different level.

Some play with alcohol and do not come back!

This is a true story: John was a successful business executive who dabbled in alcohol, but after a series of very stressful situations involving family, he lost his grip on reality. I encouraged him to attend therapy, but he stated "therapy was not for him." He defined himself as a very private person and would not share his innermost thoughts. He had been on mental health appointments and went a time or two before discontinuing treatment. Instead, he sought women, believing that the right woman could solve his problems of loneliness and loss of purpose. If only he could marry, his life would be saved.

To each relationship, he brought unrealistic expectations of how a girlfriend or wife should respond to his every need. His whole focus was based on satisfying his needs in a timely manner. Lady number one did not return his calls when he expected. Lady number two was not sexually available to meet his every need. He was too needy, desperate, and driving women away from him. John never came back from his alcohol experience, as within a year, he died alone in the privacy of his home.

Alcohol, Drugs and Eating Out

My client, Becky, went to her favorite upscale bar for salmon, salad, and wine. On her side, there was only the bartender and a regular customer, who eventually asked her out. As usual, she said no.

She had started eating her meal and then decided to go to the restroom. She left her unfinished meal and glass of wine under the watchful eye of a bartender friend and a regular at the bar. As she returned to her seat, she noticed the other side of the " L"-shaped bar was busy, and the bartender was needed on that side. She finished her drink and left without finding the bartender to say goodbye.

On her way home, she noticed a weird sensation but still felt safe to drive a few blocks. When she stopped at the traffic light, the lights looked like brightly colored candies, and she fell asleep at the light. She woke up and drove to the next block to arrive safely home. Later, she remembered the man who had asked her out more than a dozen times was seated at the end of the bar. She believes he drugged her and jokingly said, "He did a poor job of guessing her weight when he drugged her, or she would not have made it home." No, this is not funny, but she survived and laughed at what could have been a fatal mistake. Protect yourself!

Alcohol & Divorce

"Divorce also causes both men and women with no previous drinking problem to be at higher risk for the first onset of alcohol disorder. Drinking alcohol causes divorce, and divorce causes an increase in alcohol consumption. The Journal of Studies on Alcohol found that a consumption increase of 1 liter of alcohol per capita brings about an increase in the divorce rate of about 20%. (Caces, MF, et al.,4 January 2015)

As you rebuild your life, take a close look at alcohol's role in your new life. How has alcohol affected your past life, and how will it affect your future life? Think about the ideal partner for you. Does he or she consume alcohol daily, and how much consumption are you willing to live with? In the last seven years, I met many good men who would be great husbands or companions but their excess alcohol consumption was among the top reasons for discontinuing the relationships.

I was recently asked, "Aren't all alcohol treatments costly?" No! There are treatments for people with little or no money, as well! I love the organization Teen Challenge, and its services are cost-free. Donations and fundraisers fund Teen Challenge.

Because of the name "Teen Challenge," one might assume that the program is confined to teenagers. However, there are many organizations made up of wonderful people doing great work and saving lives. I have been to a couple of their events and fallen in love with the performers. I am not a specialist in these organizations, and encourage you to do your own research. Below are national hotlines to help guide you.

Reach out for confidential and compassionate services that target alcohol and substance abusers.

AA defines alcoholism as
"a physical compulsion, coupled with a mental obsession to consume alcohol."

Alcoholics Anonymous: aa.org AA's website has assessment tools and helpful steps towards recovery.

National Alliance on Mental Illness: NAMI helpline at 1-800-950-6264

Substance Abuse and Mental Health Services Administration SAMHSA 1-800-662-4357

The Veterans Administration Va.gov/contact-us/

MyVA411

1-800-698-2411

Like the rest of society, there are drugs in the dating world. Date rape drugs cause feelings of sedation and amnesia. "The most common are alcohol, marijuana, benzodiazepines, cocaine, heroin and amphetamines." Any substance that lowers sexual inhibition and possibly facilitates sexual intercourse, wanted or not. (Weir E., 2001).

Drugs can be ingested in a variety of ways, including forms - tablets, liquids, and powders can even be blown into one's nose. The time from the injection can vary from immediate to about 30 minutes.

There are multiple symptoms, and no one individual may get them all. They are not all-inclusive: Slurred speech, dizziness, feeling very drunk after one drink, unconsciousness, muscle control, nausea, confusion, memory loss, blackouts, and lower blood pressure. Vision problems, feelings of relaxation, increased sensuality, seizures, memory loss, sweating, slow heart rate, nausea and vomiting, blackouts, and loss of consciousness, including distorted perceptions of sight and sound, out-of-body or dream-like experiences, problems breathing, loss of coordination, convulsions, numbness, violent behavior, high blood pressure, and, in high doses, even death. (Cafasso, J., 19 May 2023).

National Sexual Assault Hotline that is free and confidential. 24/7 Call 800-656-HOPE

Safeguard Yourself

Protect yourself from being drugged by never taking drinks from others, opening containers yourself, watching your drink as it is poured, and never leaving your drink unattended; if you dance and leave your drink, get a fresh drink. You may know the bartender, but he cannot watch everyone in the room.

I have heard people say: If only, I had just one friend,
It might be worth trying to save myself.
I am your friend!

My friend is gone, but you are here!

You are my new friend, and I want to see you WIN!
There is a new life waiting for you to show up!
May God Bless and Keep You!
Don't give up!

Chapter 16

Don't Shoot the Wounded

BEING SINGLE IS A JOURNEY, and everyone you meet has a different timetable, depending on the number of years they have been single and their experiences. During the first year following a life event such as death or divorce, most feel lost and lonely. The sound of an empty house is overwhelming. Often, we want to find someone to save, love, and give us something or someone to belong to.

Some want to marry right away, while others want to date around because this is their first taste of freedom. In short, when we begin a single life, most are not our best selves. There is so much to learn, and seasoned singles tend not to date new singles because they are unstable and feel the need to talk about their ex. Seasoned daters don't want to listen to the saga of how you are wronged and the ex is the source of all your problems.

I had been talking to a man from the mountains for a while, so we decided to meet. He was very adamant about when and where to meet. When we met, he looked a little disheveled. His hair was untrimmed and uncombed. I let his poor grooming pass, as I grew up in the county and figured he had been working outside and had a tough morning.

TAKE NOTE!

When he or she arrives poorly groomed for the date, their preparation shows that this date was not important to them. The lack of grooming kills the prospective relationship before it has a chance to start.

We talked for a few minutes, and he told me his wife had recently died. His conversation centered on his multiple homes and assets, his well-known career, and the proximity of forest fires to his homes. Adding to his burden were the deaths of a couple of male friends over the last year or two. Now, he took on the responsibility of being the widows' handyman. He also spoke of his involvement with the people and events in the community.

In return, I told him about my life, and he interrupted, saying that this date was not all about me. I said, "Okay, please tell me more about yourself." So, he talked on. Then, from out of nowhere, he called me a "Gold Digger," saying he could recognize a "Gold Digger" a mile away as he continued to talk about himself.

He called me a "Gold Digger" for the second time. Still, I listened to what he had to say, and when he called me a

"Gold Digger" a minute later, the third time, I stood up and walked out without saying goodbye.

Embarrassed, he jumped up behind me to go to the men's room. As I looked back it was evident that he had humiliated himself as he realized the people at the surrounding tables were listening.

It is usual and customary for people at the surrounding tables to listen to conversations they perceive as dating. Spotting people on their first date is easy; they shake hands and try to communicate. For surrounding tables, listening was to us was like watching a television soap opera.

My analysis was the man seemed to be in a state of grief, and a psychiatrist could have been of more help than any date.

Finding new friends and dating is part of the transition from grieving to the dating process. Lots of people date while they are grieving because they are driven to fill the hole in their hearts, the void.

I was empathetic to his challenge. I didn't invest my heart in the first meeting, so it was no emotional heartache. I believe the first meeting is a fact-finding mission to see if there is a reason to date. Some singles are lucky and find the person of their dreams on the first date, but most do not. Dating is a numbers game; not everyone is a good fit for our lives, regardless of how handsome, beautiful, smart, or rich they are. We only need one soulmate. Don't get down on yourself because your first meeting did not work out or you think that was a failure on your part.

The meeting was just what it was, a first meeting or interview to determine if we were compatible enough to date.

A client met with a man named Fernando from an outlying town. She suggested they meet at Starbucks, and he argued that McDonald's next door was better. She said she had been thinking about a mocha frappe all morning. He was controlling and stated their date would be at McDonald's and he would buy breakfast.

The rest of the date did not improve, so she only ordered coffee and left immediately. As she drove away, he called to say he liked her body. He said a dating relationship did not require love. He offered a relationship that was sex only. She hung up and blocked him.

There are all kinds of people in the single world.
Some you will like!
Forget the rest!

Chapter 17

Scammers & Scammer Traits

Scam artists, also known as scammers, make money by tricking people for their personal information, bank accounts, and credit card numbers. In this chapter, I aim to raise awareness of scammers using social media, apps, and dating sites to meet potential partners or victims. I've had positive experiences by not allowing myself to suffer any monetary losses. I understand loneliness. When we are lonely, we risk too much of ourselves, including money and safety. Be safe!

Be prepared for suspected scam activities. Staying alert is dating safely.

IT's important to remember scammers are everywhere. They will never be your friend. They seek your money and personal information. They target various platforms, including banking, emails, social media, websites, apps, and text messages. Even dating sites are not immune to these scams.

One characteristic of a scammer is they will quickly endeavor to move your contact with them from their communication site or dating site, etc. They are trying to move you to sites that are less safe, like apps. About 40% of the scam loss reports had communication with WhatsApp, Google Chat, or Telegram. (FTC, 2003)

As you communicate with this person, your hopes and dreams are often requested, along with images of you in your bathing suit or gym clothes, even without clothing. While you might be proud of your body, beware of sending intimate photos.

Once the photos leave your hands, you will have no control over where they are displayed or how they may be used. Some people have darker reasons for wanting your photographs like sextortion.

Sextortion is the practice of using a victim's photos to threaten mass distribution on social media. The perpetrators require your payment to keep the images off the internet. "If you do pay, how long will the photos be undistributed? (FTC, 2023). Don't give away your power.

"As per the Federal Trade Commission, "sextortion reports have increased. People aged 18-29 were over six times more likely to report than those over 30. In 2022, 58% of the sextortion victims identified their contact method as being Instagram and Snapchat." (FTC.2023).

Some dating sites work hard to reject suspected bad actors. Some will tell you their online name and explain that they are no longer active. This is a case of buyer beware! Delete suspects quickly, blocking their text messages and contact information.

Despite these challenges, I maintain online social media accounts because I have found a couple of good men per year. They were good men just not a fit for my life. Reasons for the lack of "fit" include lifestyles, personalities, obligations, geography, family obligations, work travel scheduling, and physical abilities, etc. Some of those cases were differences of activity level including sports and my lack of interest or ability to perform at their level. We are still friends. This should give you hope and motivation to continue your search for genuine connections.

Scam #1. It is incredible how creative and elaborate scammers can be. A current scam targeting well-educated and wealthy people goes to the extreme of creating a corporate construction website with photographs of current and past projects.

This so-called company has offices throughout America and abroad. The perpetrator's photo is displayed in a high-rise office. The man talks to this woman several times over a couple of weeks to build a relationship. She researches his multiple businesses and finds no mention of the companies ever existed.

She told the perpetrator he was a scammer, and the

website came down a few days later. My client reports no further contact with the man.

Scam #2. Another popular scam involves a man posing as an Alaskan fisherman getting ready to retire. He has determined that you are unique and wants to care for you for the rest of your life. As the story goes, there is trouble with his ship's propeller due to hitting a small iceberg. He is in Anchorage and must stay with the ship until it is repaired, so he cannot meet you according to your original arrangements later this week. His best-case timing means he cannot meet you for several weeks. As a result of the layover, he has no money and asks you to send him $500.00, as he lost his debit card. He explains that your money is not at risk because he will pay you back when he sees you.

Scam #3. An elderly woman named Sarah is a victim of an ongoing scam. Although warned of being a victim, she continues to talk to a man multiple times per week over the course of months. Last I heard, she had given the scammer $50,000. She is of sound mind and believes the companionship is worth it, as she is financially secure.

Scam #4. The scammer has a photo that looks similar to a TV broadcaster. He has been conversing with a woman for over a few weeks and offers many ideas, including places to eat in her town. He states he is from a small town and rattles off that her city is exactly 25 miles away and close enough to consider a relationship with him. He names some historical sites, including restaurants, and tries to blend into that community virtually.

The scammer's knowledge of your location and the idea that he is from a small town are designed to comfort you, making you think he's a neighbor or country boy.

He mentions they should meet at a national donut franchise and provides cross streets. Scammers disarm unsuspecting victims by claiming to live in small towns near their city. This practice inspires a sense of trust. Knowing the exact mileage for many small towns surrounding the victim's city is suspicious. His ability to refer to exact mileage means nothing by itself but coupled with a few other traits, it might identify him as a scammer. The potential victims quit communicating.

Scam #5. I had been talking to a man from a small town just outside my large city. He was supposedly a miner working out of state and would return the following week to love and care for me for the rest of my life.

Oddly enough," I was walking into a medical center for tests when my phone accidentally called him on FaceTime. He answered, and I could see him as I remembered. Only next to him were men in matching shirts with computers and phones in front of them. This looked like an organized call center since they were all talking romance. I confronted him and hung up.

Scam #6. A female dating prospect has inherited millions from her father's estate and needs to travel to countries where women have no rights. Therefore, she needs to get engaged before leaving America. Her engagement and a letter from this man's attorney will give her the legal power to inherit.

She needs money for travel and to pay an attorney to represent her while claiming her inheritance. Then she promises to come home to you and be your loving wife. The lady even sent a contract claiming the man was her fiancé and requested he read, sign, and send money. Don't laugh. I know a smart, well-educated man who took the documents to his attorney to determine the contract's validity before he sent the money. Originally, the intended victim planned to send his money before meeting with the attorney.

Other Scamming Characteristics

Most scams are grandiose, bigger than life, and too good to be true.

JOBS: These scam artists have extravagant jobs requiring them to travel frequently out of the country. They may also be retired or wealthy and have jobs in engineering and architecture, mining, medicine, nursing, etc.

PHOTOS: Scammer photos show a happy life with lots of recreational travel, including dogs, cats, babies, and a big luxurious house.

The photography often looks different. Bright and blown out, with unusual cars and styles parked on the wrong side of the street. Look at the high-rise buildings displayed in the background. Scammers often disproportionately display lots of European cities. Look at the clothing and unusual street materials, including brick roadways. No one of these traits makes a person a scammer, but when coupled with other distinctive traits, take notice. Consider the percentage of people who travel to other countries and compare to the profile. Question every situation. What is different about the photo?

TEXTING: There are scammers worldwide. Sometimes, you do not reach the intended gender. It is reported some countries use little boys to solicit men as well. True or not it is possible. Many scammers don't spell well or use words correctly or use British English. For example, words like favor in American English lack the "u" of European spelling **favour**.

Before texting a potential date, I check for legitimacy. I often ask Google if this phone or text number has been involved in scamming or criminal activity. It's quick and free, but paid background checks are more effective. Free information does not come with the same level of accuracy. When I have a high level of interest and enough information, I sometimes do a background check. I also will call back the texting number to see if an answering service answers.

Texting an answering service is not bad by itself; I say put all data in the virtual backpack when a series of abnormal circumstances don't add up make a decision to move on. Tread carefully.

PHONE CALLS: Listen for hoarseness or accents, as well as English being a second language.

Phone calls often go to nondescript answering services. Does the voice sound older or younger than the person portrays? Consider how callers listen but don't understand, which causes you to restate the conversation frequently. Their voice sounds off and they make excuses like having a cold, just woke up, or whatever.

COMMON OCCURRENCES: Scammers always need money for someone sick, hurt, or jailed. They offer to teach you how to invest and have conversations like, "Let's talk about marriage," "I've come into some money," etc.

The scammer's preferred payment methods include cryptocurrency, bank wire transfer or payment, gift cards, and payment from an app or service.

Always be skeptical of circumstances that are too good to be true.

Are you guilty of falling in love, or enamored with the idea of being in love

We must save ourselves!

Chapter 18

Roadmaps, Rainbows, & Pots of Gold

As we conclude this book, you should have a better understanding of the single life, dating, intimacy, romance, sexuality, and physical challenges that come with age for both men and women. You have found that healing from past relationships takes time to focus on yourself and the future. You must take the first steps to heal your mind, body, and soul. You've discovered healthy ways to increase your confidence and found new people and places to hang out.

When I take the first step on faith, the Lord always gives me direction and shows me where the next step should be. It's an adventure requiring trust. When my daughter was young, I told her, "You must travel this path, but that does not mean that you have to feel every bump in the road. Look above the trees because that is where you will find your destination. Don't internalize your challenges and allow them to hurt you; they are only temporary. You will overcome!"

You have also seen samples of active scams designed to take advantage of you and your money. These scams seek your personal information, including your address, credit card, name, and money. Recognizing scammers means listening and scrutinizing everything you learn about them. They often differ in their spoken and printed language, as well as their photography styles.

You now have an awareness of the scammer's mode of operations. Tools have been provided in the form of sample fraud to identify scams before you lose your money or security. Remember, everything in their game is always bigger and better than the real world, from the majestic jobs, locations, and travel destinations to how they will save you from your life and love for you forever.

Practicing safety includes being watchful of new people coming into your life. Take your time before sharing your address, which could mean not allowing the date to pick you up for the first date or two. And never share your finances and bank account information.

You have grieved your old relationships, endured the pain of hearing the empty house, and plotted a new course with the help of assessment tools. You have planted the flag between your old life and new life, representing where you have been and your progress from that point.

The data from assessment tools will soon affirm that you are getting your life on track and headed in the right direction. In the event that you are still struggling, seek professional help in the form of a doctor of psychology or psychologist.

In the future, you can track your improvement between your old life and new life. These tools can also be used to measure a future partner's fit in your life, as well.

The assessments have served as a road map from where you began this trek. The information became relevant the day you planted your flag and viewed your life 360 degrees. Consideration has been given to the roles you play in your family, the jobs you work, the status of your emotions, health, physical condition, career, finances, obligations, and responsibilities to family, your interests, faith, views on your old life, and more.

Once your 360 was identified and you saw all facets of yourself at a moment's notice, you moved forward to focus and forgive yourself with a plan. You have moved forward with a plan to focus and forgive yourself. You have found clarity by defining your likes, dislikes, and dreams for your new life. Your schedule is starting to sort out and become more of a routine.

You have decided whether you want to date and established personal and dating goals. These goals include self-improvement and dating preparation, such as grooming and clothing styles to build a new wardrobe.

Your assessment profile defines the kind of person you are and want to be. This process has improved the "New You." You have built confidence and a new attitude. Fine grooming and clothing have helped you regain confidence.

You have rid yourself of the hatred that caused you to stumble, thus forgiving yourself and others. You are reminded that moving forward in life is nearly impossible without forgiveness. You gained confidence by getting involved with people, life, faith, and charities that fit your lifestyle.

Your life has new forms of entertainment and sporting activities, like pickleball, tennis, golf, clubs, singles groups, and dancing. Being involved in life has given you a way to cope with the silence of the empty house and a new purpose that is unique to you.

Realizing life and health changes are a part of life is not as stressful since you understand you are not alone in your sexual struggles. The enjoyment of romance and intimacy is exciting at any age. It is up to us to cope, understand, and overcome the setbacks of Menopause and Erectile Dysfunction with creativity. By now, you have gotten professional help with medical and sexual issues.

Your New Love

As you approach your new love, prioritize yourself and your mate. Don't blend your family until you **really, really** believe this is the one. They don't want to know the succession of your dates. When you involve children, be they young or old, in selecting a new mate, you are allowing family and friends to judge you and your relationship, which will affect your future.

When we involve our children too soon, we give them a voice in our decision to love or be loved. We don't need their influence on what the heart wants. They do not lie lonely in bed night after night.

To find happiness, do something for others. You cannot make yourself happy, and doing for others allows you to see the smiling faces in the lives you made better.

"God grant me the **serenity**
To **Accept** the things I cannot change.
Courage to change the things I can,
And **Wisdom** to know the difference."

Chapter 19

Bonus Chapter: My Dating Stories

MOST OF MY *dates were good, we just were not a good fit for one another's lives.*

This date was different, as Charles and I had dated a few times for dinner at local restaurants. Charles invited me for a BBQ at his house. We ate and lounged on the couch watching TV. After a few hours he tried to take my pants off and would not stop grabbing at my clothes. I said no repeatedly.

I ran to the door only to find that the door would not open. I tried to open the door the second time and the door was stuck. Finally, I pulled with all my might, the door opened.

While I was tugging at the door, I was anxious and the hair on my neck stood on end. Finally, I was in my car and drove off. I never talked with him again, but have noticed that he is still on dating sites and sending friend requests to my Facebook. Women, this is a case of buyer be-ware!

Control

Six or seven years ago, my boyfriend and I were talking about getting married. He wanted to buy me a new Navigator and a huge diamond ring.

We had discussed keeping my home and that he would sell his home in three years when his current job would be finished. The plan was for him to move to my home town.

As time went on, he decided that we should sell my house and invest the money. He wanted to trade my car in on the Navigator.

When we were at his house the temperature was set at 69 and I froze. As time went on, this was just one more of his controlling behaviors. He purposely froze me so that I would sleep closer to him. Other skills he thought I needed to learn included the correct way to pour laundry detergent into the washer.

My knee was popping out and I needed a replacement. We planned for him to take care of me in my home for the first week post-surgery. And later stay at his house enabling him to take me to physical therapy in the following weeks. The plan included receiving my physical therapy within two blocks from his house.

Then came the Sunday afternoon, while I was preparing for knee surgery on Monday. Victor said helping me was asking too much and walked out of door. Then, I was without someone to take care of me, and the hospital would not allow the surgery. As per the doctor, I would be on heavy pain medications and needed someone to manage my meds.

Now what? Surgery was scheduled in twelve hours and mom was out of town, so I had no plan "B" to meet the surgical deadline. As I was saying good bye to my ex-fiancé on the driveway, upset and weeping, my neighbor had witnessed my devastation and wanted to help. I shared that I could not have surgery to be free from pain without surgery. She said that she would get me to surgery and we will work out the long-term details, as we went along.

That evening a special friend, an ex-boyfriend called to see if I needed anything. What a sweet heart, he offered to take care of me for the following a week until mom got home. He took a week off work and gave me thoughtful care.

For taking care of me on the days when I shook from pain, he paid a personal price. He lost his girlfriend, as she was upset that he stayed and gave me 24-hour care for the week.

God provided me answers where there were none. Thank God for planting great people in my path.

Though it was painful losing my ex-fiancé, it was a blessing. He demonstrated the need control by advising me how to put soap in the washer. His freezing me out of his home was calculative and designed for his own pleasure. He came first, proven by his lack of care and flexibility in my time of need.

Think of where I would be today if we had proceeded with the marriage. My personal car would have been gone and the equity would have been entangled in the transaction on the new Navigator. As well as, my home would have been gone and the proceeds from the sale would have been intertwined with investment accounts.

With no car, no home, no money, no choices, I could have been locked into his life and challenged to meet his every need, his way.

Thank you, JESUS!

Some religions and ideologies are not compatible, no matter how much you care for the person.

I had been talking to a fella named Dale from the mountains for several weeks. We had enjoyed one another's phone conversations. After a few weeks we decided to meet for coffee. As I was driving to meet him, he called and suggested since he was driving forty-five minutes to town, he wanted dinner.

He chose a great place for dinner. Along the way, our conversation came up regarding religion and how we lived our lives. He was an atheist and loved to spend his late evening and early morning playing rock music. I am a Christian, go to bed at 9 pm, and love a quiet home. Thus, we could not ever be compatible.

I told him that I could not fulfill his needs as a girlfriend or wife. My direct conversation was "I cannot fulfill your wants, needs, and desires." As I revealed that I was a Christian and could not allow him penetrate me in anyway. No kissing and no physical relationship could be found between us.

He got really mad, stating that he was rich, brilliant, and could solve any problems that life brought his way. He stated he did not need an old man to use as a crutch. He was referring to Jesus Christ, as the old man.

With that, I stood up and began to walk out of the restaurant. He stopped me saying that I owed for my meal. I said "look I would have been happy to pay for my coffee at our original location, however, you decided to come for a fancy dinner, the tab is yours BIG BOY!"

Be mindful of safety issues and unsolicited attention by the opposite sex.

Over the course of my single life, I've had three stalkers and three peeping Toms. There was a stalker in my neighborhood who had been watching me from his room over the patio and called to tell me so. Then I was driving the freeway on my way out of town for work when he passed me. I ran into him later in the laundry room and told him if I'd heard from him again, I would call the police.

Coincidently, his wife noticed him paying too much attention to me, my where a-bouts, and demanded that they move.

* * *

I REGULARLY WALKED around my community on a daily basis. Sometimes neighbors invited me for coffee on their verandas. Nice! I was walking my normal routine and a single man invited me for coffee on the veranda.

As I walked past his home the next day he offered me coffee again, and again. He was good conversationalist, then I found out that he was setting his alarm clock so coffee was ready for my routine walk. That creeped me out and was too much attention so I changed my routine.

Singles are a lonely bunch, no harm and no foul.

Smoking and Hearing can affect relationships.

I dated a very nice man for a while. He was a chain smoker, and I did not smoke.

He always insisted on driving his vehicle that seemed to be a smoking lounge. He thought that rolling down the window and smoking was a compromise. However, I have allergies and don't handle cigarette smoke very well. My goal was to drive my car without smoking. Try as I might, I could not get past his smoking.

His smoking was tough, but he also had hearing issues. I tried to get him to get tested for hearing aids, but he was insulted. Watching television one night on maximum volume broke the speakers on my new TV.

His lack of effort regarding his smoking and not seeking help with his hearing reminded me that he came first. This proved I was unimportant to him. At that point I wished him well but had no interest in creating a lifelong relationship.

Later I got my hearing checked and found I could hear the fan situated on the outside of the soundproof room. The staff said I had the very best hearing they had ever tested.

Peeping Toms

I caught my neighbor peeking into my living room on more than one occasion. One time his phone went off while he was leaning next to my window alarming me that he was watching.

I went into my back yard and saw him climbing out of my flower bed. Recognized him as my backyard neighbor. He was in his 80's and smaller in stature than myself. As I rounded the corner of my home. He grabbed my arm.

I told him if I caught him again, I would beat him up and call the police. Probably not the smartest way to approach a man who peeks. I was armed with a stun gun and the situation defused quickly.

I later mention his behavior to some of the neighborhood ladies and they said he cannot do much harm, let him enjoy himself. I was snarky and asked what time they would like to be displayed in the window of their homes for his pleasure.

Acknowledgments

Advisors

Barb Dotta, Steve Vuyovich, Steve Serpa, Gordon Kost

Dry Creek Alumni

My classmates who have believed and encouraged me for most of my life

Dorothy and the Cline Family

For helping me when I was too sick to help myself.

Valley Writers Group (VWG)

The group of wonderful writers & editors who encouraged me with their honesty

Erectile Dysfunction Board (ED)

Who bravely shared their innermost symptoms, and feelings, named Chapter 14

Erectile Dysfunction, "Hurdle & Not A Barrier"

The men wish to remain anonymous,

To create openness and understanding for both men and women affected by ED

To make a platform for open discussions

Assuring men and women that they are not alone in their struggle

Editor

Joan Raymond

Photographer

Tom Milne: https://milnephotography.com

Cover Designer

Isharit Fared

Friend & Professional Consultant

Beth Bridges Brandle

Bibliography

Breiding MJ, et al. (2014). Prevalence and characteristics of sexual violence, stalking, and intimate partner violence victimization-National Intimate partner and sexual violence survey, United States, 2011. www.cdc.gov/mmwr/preview/mmwrhtml/ss6308a1.htm Accessed 11/10/24

Brenner, GH MD, DFAPA. Fagan, Abigail (March 6, 2021). "Why Men Need to Feel Desired"

Accessed November 9,2024. (psychology today.cm/us/blog/experimentations/202103/why-men-need-to-feel-desired). (Psychology Today) https:www.psychologytoday.com>sex-socialbility."

Caces, M. F., Harford, T. C., Williams, G. D., & Hanna, E. Z. (1999). Alcohol consumption and divorce rates in the United States. *Journal of studies on alcohol*, 60(5), 647–652. https://doi.org/10.15288/jsa.1999.60.647

Cafasso, Jacquelyn, Carter A. Pharm.D Medical Review. "Symptoms and Effects of Date Rape Drugs. Healthline.com/health/date-rape-drugs

Calm. (n.d.)., Calm. Mosunic, PhD, RD,MBA, "Think you're dating a beta male? Here's what it means" November19, 2024. https//www.calm.com

Dodgson, Lindsay (23 Jan 2018).https://www.businessinsider.com/why-empaths-and-narcissists-are-attracted-to-each-other-2018-1 (accesses March 15,2025).

Fair, Lesley. (13 February 2024). "Love Stinks" https://www.ftc.gov/business-guidance/blog/2024/02/love-stinks-when-scammer-involved_(accessed March 15,2025).

Gillette, H. (2022, July 1). "Dominant Personality: Traits, Behaviors, and How to Handle" Medically Reviewed by, Gepp, Karin. Psyd.(July 1, 2022) Accessed October 15, 2024.

Jefferson, Thomas, "If you want, you've never had; you must be willing to do something you've never done." Accessed, October 1, 2024. Berkes, Anna: 2/13/2013 Monticello.org/research-education/Thomas-Jefferson-encyclopedia. Earliest known appearance in print: 2004: 2012, This quote has not been found in any of the writings of Thomas Jefferson

Johnson TC, MD. (April 23, 2023), Medically Reviewed by WebMD Editorial Contributors. https://www.webmd.com>Sexual Health>Birth Control. (Accessed Nov. 10, 2024)

Khan, Lima M., Chair of the Federal Trade Commission, "Romance scammers' favorite lies exposed." Ftc/gpvmews-events/data-visualizations/data-spotlight/2023/02/romance-scammers-favorite-lies-exposed. (Accessed November 8, 2023).

Kaskutas L.A. (2009). (Alcoholics Anonymous effectiveness: faith meets science. "Journal of addictive diseases, 28 (2), 145-157 https://doi. org/10.1080/10508809027724.64

Lawrenz, Lori, PsyD. Moore, Marissa, April 5, 2022 "The Difference between mourning and grieving" PsychCentral: Downloaded 10/24/2023

Leslie SW, & Sooriyamoothy, T. Erectile Dysfunction. [updated 2024 January 9]. In: StatPearls (Internet). Treasure Island (FL): StatPearls Publishing: 2024 Jan. Available from: https://www.ncbi.nih.gov/ books/NBK562253/

Lewis, J. (2023, January 11). The alpha male explained: 9 true signs you're an alpha male. *Zellalife*. Accessed 10/9/2024. https://www. zellalife.com/blog/the-alpha-male-explained-9-true-signs-youre-an-alpha-male/

Bibliography

Louis Armstrong. (2020, November 18). *Louis Armstrong- What a Wonderful World* [*Official Video*]. YouTube. https://www.youtube.com/watch?v=CWzrABouyeE.

lyrics.com/lyric/250311/Whitney+Houston/Greatest+Love+of+All accessed 10/14/2024. Written by Linda Creed, Michael Masser Lyrics@Sony/ATV Music Publishing LLC. Lyrics Licensed & Provided by LyricFind

Mass.gov/info-details/recognizing-the-signs-of-unhealthy-relationships, the 2023 Commonwealth of Massachusetts. 9/26/2023. Accessed October 15, 2024.

Merriam-webster.com/dictionary/confidence 8/28/2023 "Confidence, Assurance, Self-Possession, Aplomb"

Marjorie Mason Center, https://mmcenter.org, Fresno CA., Accessed 10/18/23

National Cancer Institute, (9 July 2024) "Grief, Bereavement, and Loss" Accessed 10/16/2024.

The National Institute of Health, Accessed 26 October 27.
https://www.niddk.nih.gov/health-information/urologic-diseases/erectile-dysfunction/symptoms- causes

University of Utah. (Accessed October 27, 2024)
https://healthcare.utah.edu/mens-health/conditions/erectile-dysfunction/trimix-injection

New International Version Bible (1978). *The Holy Bible, New International Version. Zondervan.*
(*Original work published 1973*), (Philippians 4:13) "I can do all things thru Christ who strengthens me".

PNAS Vol 117 No. 31 pnas.org/doi/10.1073/pnas.2000158117 "Behavioral traits that define social dominance are the same that reduce social influence in a consensus task".

Sanfordbehaviouralhealth.com/2021/05/25/alcohol-divorce-drinking-ruining-marriage/
https://stanfordbehavioralhealth.com/2021/05/25/alcohol-divorce-thinking-ruining-marriage/

Stanford Medical Center, (2017, March 17), Friedrich Nietzsche,
http://plato.stanford.edu>entries>nietzshhe "It is not a lack of love, but a lack of friendship that makes unhappy marriages." Accessed August 9, 2023

U.S. Immigration and Customs Enforcement. (2025, February 8). Romance scams -Protectyourself. ICE.https://.www.ice.gov (accessed March 15, 2025)

VA.Gov/health-care/health-needs-conditions/substance-use-problems "Substance use treatment for Veterans." Accessed: 3, November, 2024.

Weir E. (2001), Drug-facilitated date rape. *CMAJ : Canadian Medical Association Journal = journal de 1'Assocation medicale canadienne,* *165(1), 80. (Accessed 5,November 2024)*

About The Author

Lynn Lasso

Lynn is deeply passionate about people, a dedication reflected in her career, charities, and education. She specializes in empowering and motivating of individuals to see success beyond what they deemed possible. She helps others to recognize their strengths, talents, and potential to move forward in life. Throughout her career, she has held diverse leadership roles including a corporate President,

Speaker & Communication Specialist, and Marketing Representative for International Companies.

Beyond her professional work, Lynn is committed to giving back. She actively volunteers, helping charities, mentoring and speaking in high schools and colleges working with students to develop career paths.

After a near death experience, she created proven steps and behavioral changes that help those singles with broken lives to regain a sense of self-worth. Although Lynn has worn many hats her favorites are family, friends, and cowgirl.

Lynn's life, education, and career supports the growth of people and companies.
She's passionate about helping people to build better lives through her book, coaching, and speaking.

For more information, contact her via her coaching website: LynnLasso.com

www.ingramcontent.com/pod-product-compliance
Lightning Source LLC
Chambersburg PA
CBHW071300130626
46556CB00003B/1408

* 9 7 9 8 9 9 2 3 9 5 1 0 5 *